# Veterans' Voices

## COVENTRY'S UNSUNG HEROES OF THE SECOND WORLD WAR

## CAROLINE FREEMAN-CUERDEN

**ISIS**
LARGE PRINT
Oxford

First published in Great Britain 2005
by
Sutton Publishing Limited

Published in Large Print 2007 by ISIS Publishing Ltd.,
7 Centremead, Osney Mead, Oxford OX2 0ES
by arrangement with
Sutton Publishing Limited

**British Library Cataloguing in Publication Data**
Veterans' voices: Coventry's unsung heroes of the
Second World War. – Large print ed.
(Isis reminiscence series)
1. World War, 1939–1945 – Personal narratives,
English
2. Large type books
3. Coventry (England) – Biography
I. Freeman-Cuerden, Caroline
940.5'481'42498

ISBN 978–0–7531–9420–1 (hb)
ISBN 978–0–7531–9421–8 (pb)

Printed and bound in Great Britain by
T. J. International Ltd., Padstow, Cornwall

Dedicated to the memory of Charlie Brown,
Arthur Mills, Grace Golland, Les Haymes,
Dennis Wood, Reg Farmer, Jim Laurie,
Gordon Batt, Benjamin Carless, Enid Barley,
Mary Alcock, Les Ryder, Thomas Horsfall; and
Catherine Collins and Esther Shapland,
who both survived the blitz.

# Contents

# Acknowledgements

A special thank you to James Cuerden, who interviewed some of the veterans in this book. Thanks also to Alan Roberts and Alan Hartley for the extra help they gave me in this project and to the following veterans: John Shuttleworth, Dennis Knight, Vick Wimbush, Sid Gardiner, Walter Throne, Mr A. Butcher, Ron Hadley, Les Porter, Roy Lewis, Les Ives, Joe Knatt, G. Cuddon. Thank you to Coventry's Burma Star Association and Navy Association for putting up with James and me at their meetings on occasion, and to Evelyn Carless, Michael Carless, Linda Case, Mike Hurn, Richard Bailey, Robert Wilkinson and all the wives who have been so helpful. To those veterans who trusted me with precious photographs, logbooks and diaries (especially you, Jack Forrest) thank you so much, and lastly, thank you for your patience Alexander, Poppy and Alice.

# Introduction

*Bridge on the River Kwai*, *The Dam Busters*, *Pearl Harbor*, we've all watched them. We've seen bullets shoot off helmets and bombs drop on homes. While Tom Hanks dodged the Germans in *Saving Private Ryan*, we ate our popcorn and learnt all about the horror of battle. We see war on the news all the time. We know what it's like.

Do we? How does it feel to join up, to get the letter that tells you you're being called up, to leave your girlfriend, your wife, for years? What was it like to lose your friends, to get hit by a mortar bomb, to see a man die, to see your first dead body, to bury one? How about when it all ended and you came home and tried to settle down? What's it like now to live with the memories?

My aim in this book was to discover and document the stories of the men and women based in and around Coventry who served in the Second World War. Some people were reluctant to talk, others more willing; many had never recounted much of their story, even to their own family and a lot couldn't understand why I would be interested. As one veteran said to me, "You know the programme *Only Fools and Horses* when that chap says 'I remember the war', and everyone tells him to shut up? Well, I used to feel like that."

I spent a lot of Saturdays in Coventry Central

Library sifting through old newspapers and tracing several veterans from articles printed sixty or so years ago. Sadly, when checking on the Commonwealth War Graves Commission website, I would discover that many of the people I was attempting to contact, particularly Coventry airmen, had been killed later in the war. Sometimes I struck lucky. I found a 1944 story of a Coventry girl who had received a medal for carrying on her duty under fire. I traced this girl who was now eighty-one and living in Wyken, Coventry.

"Hello, is that Grace Golland? I'm sorry to bother you. You don't know me but I'm researching a local history book on Coventry's Second World War veterans and I found an article about you in an old 1944 newspaper. I wondered if you wouldn't mind talking to me some time."

"How did you get this number?" a very brusque voice asked me.

"I looked up the Gollands in the phone book and by chance tracked down your sister."

"Well, she shouldn't have given you my number. Who are you anyway? A journalist?"

"No, I'm not a journalist . . ."

"A student?"

"I'm just a mother and I'm interested in your story; I think it's important what you did. I've spoken to lots of men but not many women. I don't think your story should be forgotten."

"Well, I'll have to think about it. I'll let you know."

About thirty minutes later Grace called me back. "I've thought about what you said, and I will talk to you." A few days later I sat in Grace's living room while she searched out her medal for me from an old drawer and told me what it was like meeting the King and tracking German planes.

Some veterans wondered if they had a story at all. "I wasn't a hero," they'd say, and they'd tell me, almost apologetically, how their war was an easy one. I was told over and over, "it was our job, someone had to do it".

Those who volunteered joined up for different reasons. Some were spurred into action by Coventry's blitz, some followed a brother, a friend, for one woman it was an escape from her father; others pursued a passion for aircraft or a love of ships. Sometimes when veterans spoke to me I felt an underlying sadness hidden inside them, perhaps in the way a man raised his shoulders and breathed out a quiet sigh, a sense of loss for ambitions or dreams put to one side while men and women went to play their part in the war. "We gave up six years of our lives. I lost the wonderful opportunity of university."

It seemed to me that the people I spoke to were from a generation who had to simply, in their own words, "just get on with it". Many still suffer nightmares and some, more than sixty years on, wiped away tears as they remembered and spoke of lost lives. As one man said to me, "Nowadays counsellors talk to everybody. With us, there was no such thing."

Among the discomfort, hardships and moments of boredom punctuated by action, there was always the comradeship. To many, coming back from war, from a life spent with mates, away from home and family, it was a tremendous adjustment to fit back into civilian life and more than a few missed the special bonds of friendship which had built up during the war years. "When I came out I missed the enormous brotherhood," one D-Day veteran told me. Another admitted, "It was more difficult coming back to Coventry than going into the Navy."

Those who came back from Burma had their own, extra difficulties to contend with. As Charlie Brown, a Coventry soldier who had fought in the war with Japan, told me, "there were no flags or welcome. We just came home in dribs and drabs. I didn't even have any money for my train fare. The guard at the station said if the inspector got on I'd have to get off. He did get on and I left the train. I didn't mind. I just wanted to see my family."

Having attended some of the meetings of the various veterans' associations in the city and seeing the camaraderie and support among the members, I realise the great value of these groups. Associations such as the Burma Star offer veterans the chance to keep hold of that feeling of comradeship. For a few, now elderly, perhaps widowed and living alone, a monthly visit to the Navy or RAF Associations may be their only social life.

It was on 15 August that I attended such a gathering. A scattering of elderly men in smart blazers cluster outside the doorway of St Margaret's Church in Ball Hill, Coventry. They are shaking hands, familiar faces, but fewer of them each year. These are the men of the

Burma Star Association, here to mark the anniversary of the end of the war with Japan and remember their dead comrades. One of them, a Sean Connery type with silver hair and moustache, leads me in and introduces me to the vicar, Lydia. "We keep her in work burying us all!" he jokes.

As the service starts the Association's standard is marched solemnly down the aisle. Ernie Sherriff reads from the Bible, and as I look at him I think of his story and imagine him in his bomber wearing his lucky elephant badge flying above the ocean, plane swooping over sharks. I look around at other elderly men and their stories also come to mind. I picture one parachuting into the jungle, explosives strapped to his body; another waking from a nightmare, brushing non-existent snakes from his bed. We sing "Amazing Grace", veterans, widows, grown-up sons and daughters all huddled together in the small chapel. The Last Post is sounded, I look across at the roll of honour, at the names of the dead carved into the Burma teak. I feel sad as I wonder if this service will even exist in ten years. The feeling of warmth and friendship is strong. The veterans care about each other, they take time to remember.

To many of us, as we busy around talking into mobile phones, dashing in and out of shops and offices, elderly men like these are just a few old blokes; what do they know about life? If we stopped to ask we would perhaps get some small insight into just what they did all those years ago. The vicar turns to me before I leave: "It's an important job — documenting it all. Someone should listen." Here are the stories of some of them.

# PART ONE

# IN THE ARMY NOW

# You Won't Hear the Shell that Gets You

## *The Story of Albert Dunn*

Albert Dunn was the youngest of five sons, all of whom joined the Army. Albert was a driver for the Royal Army Service Corps and served at Dunkirk, in the Middle East and North Africa. His account focuses on his experiences at Dunkirk when he was just a young man of nineteen.

I was the youngest brother out of the lot and they really looked after me. I was always interested in warships and I wanted to join the Navy but my dad wouldn't allow it. In 1926, when I was just six years old, he was working on a submarine, which was above the water and still in dock. For some reason or other it suddenly sank and six men were killed. My father lost his index finger. When I wanted to join the Navy he said, "No way. You'll join the Army."

So all us boys ended up in the Army. It was the first time I'd ever left them when I had to go to Dunkirk. I was a driver; I went through the whole war driving trucks, and when I came out I had to pass a driving test, would you believe, after all those years.

3

When we first got to France we were in one big street, trucks all lined up from one end to the other. We had different jobs to go to. I remember going to Vimy Ridge, which the Canadians had stormed in the First World War, and there were still shells sticking out of the trenches.

I had to get rid of my lorry on the way to Dunkirk, destroy it so the Germans couldn't use it. You just pulled over to the edge of the road, put a brick on the accelerator, opened up the radiator and let the vehicle run dry. We followed behind all the evacuees; we didn't know where we were being sent next and had no idea we would be sent home.

I stayed on the beach waiting for three nights and two days. We had no food. They were strafing the men, shelling us, planes coming over, Stuka dive-bombers coming down on us. You can imagine what we felt. I tripped up on an Army boot which was lying on the beach at one point. When I looked down at it there was a man's foot inside. I could still cry about that. You never forget.

I prayed a lot and I have to admit I did cry. People can call you a baby but you had to be there: the bombing, the shelling, ships sinking and smoking. How could you get out of it? We didn't know what was going to happen. We'd dig ourselves into the sand dunes for cover, but you had to come out to queue up and get off the beach. We all stood in line together, officers mixed in with us waiting their turn the same as every man. There you'd be all lined up and the Germans would come, planes flying over you machine-gunning, shells exploding. You just had to run back into the dunes again. We slept in those dunes at night, dug right in, no protection or cover over us and sometimes they would shell at night. It was terrifying.

They say you won't hear the shell that gets you. When we were making our way across the beach the shells were landing as usual. The lad next to me looked at a crater where one had just hit. "It never hits the same place twice," he said to me and he leapt in there for protection. A shell came over and landed right on top of him, blew his arm off. I'll never forget him till my dying day. He was crying out, "Please help me, please help me." I wanted to stop but some medics came up and told me to move on.

Towards the end the German planes dropped all these leaflets telling us to surrender. We didn't bother with that. I remember one German who got shot down. His plane hit the water; you could hear the engines roaring as it went in. He parachuted out but he didn't stand a chance. He was shot to pieces by machine-guns before he hit the sea.

There were quite a few men drowned as they queued up in the water and tried to wade out to the boats. I couldn't swim myself. You'd line up and people at the back would push forward, so you had no choice. You couldn't do anything about it, you had to move forward and there were men went under. A lot of people were trying to bring their gear back with them too and that just wasn't possible. I came back with nothing whatsoever, not even my tin hat.

I was lifted into the boat by these two sailors. I was absolutely exhausted, I just collapsed. They took my rifle off me, took out the bolt, threw that over one side of the boat and the rifle over the other, straight into the sea. They wanted to make more room for the men. I went back over to Dunkirk after the war and there used to be a shop that sold all the equipment, rifles and stuff that they'd picked up off the beach. I always remember when I eventually got on board HMS *Golden Eagle*, they gave me bully beef, biscuits and hot cocoa.

There were smaller boats coming out to the ship. They had to be winched up and the men taken off. That was all too slow so we started pulling the ropes by hand to get the boats up faster. It was exhausting, we were so dead beat. The Germans started shelling the ship and we had to up-anchor and go out into deeper water. When we came back in to pick up more men, all those little boats had gone and I never did know what happened to them.

When I got back to England it was to a place called Mansfield and I stayed the night at a school. The locals brought blankets and things and we slept on the floor. There was a barber over the road and he was giving all the men free haircuts. Three weeks later and I was posted somewhere else. I never got a medal for being in France because you had to be there for six months and I just missed that. I never got a medal for Dunkirk either because they said they didn't give them for a retreat.

The friendship in the Army was a great thing; it was the biggest thing of all really. You all got to live together and you could all die together. That's the way we used to look at it. Dunkirk was a different experience altogether. You knew what you were going through and what all the other lads were living through. You thought to yourself, "Well that's it" and you said your prayers. When I can't sleep sometimes, even more than sixty years after Dunkirk, I think back to that time. My wife will stay up chatting to me and I'll talk about those days and the things I saw, and I can still get upset even now I'm eighty-five.

# It Nearly Killed Us but We Were Fit as Fleas

## The Story of Dennis Wood

Dennis Wood joined the Army when he was seventeen, just before war was declared. He served in home defence at postings all over Britain.

My dad was in the Navy in the First World War, so listening to stories from him and his old shipmates I wanted to go to sea, the same as him. There was a two-day medical for that. I got through the first day all right but then failed on eyesight. I didn't know I had a weak eye, I didn't wear glasses or anything. When I got rejected by the Navy I tried the Army. I went down to Queen's Road recruitment office; they sent me home, told me to come back nine o'clock sharp the next morning when I took the oath and was presented with the King's shilling. I was in the Army.

I was told I was in the Royal Warwicks and I thought that's a good local regiment, I shall be off to Budbrooke Barracks. Afraid not. They sent me to Aldershot. There were three of us from Coventry. We travelled together and when we got there we were taken to this hut and told that this would be our home until there was a sufficiency of us to make up a platoon.

This bugle sounded out and we were told this was the cookhouse call and to make our way there straightaway. We had no knives or forks, nothing at all. We were in civilian clothes and there were a lot of catcalls from all the blokes in fatigues. We were taken to this table for recruits, which was right at the far end of the dining hall, and we were shunned. It was like that meal after meal. After a few meals other recruits started to come into our hut, civilian lads like me, and after about a fortnight there was quite a collection of us. We still didn't have anything; we couldn't have a shave, we got a wash occasionally if we could hang out where the ablutions were and some kind squaddie would lend us his soap and his towel. That was the way we carried on. We were in a right state, not a clean shirt between us.

Eventually an orderly officer came into the hut and said there were now enough of us and to follow him to the quartermaster's stores. We were issued with our kit at last and I ended up with a kitbag full of clothes. I had a stiff cap, highly polished peak, tunic with shiny buttons, Royal Warwicks badges on the lapel, Army boots and a swagger cane with a shiny knob on the end. After six or seven weeks more men joined, we became a platoon and then a company.

One day we were ordered to go to a certain point in the barracks. They'd rigged up these loudspeakers and they told us there was going to be an important announcement by Neville Chamberlain. It came over on the system that war had been declared with

Germany. We didn't know what it meant really. Everything felt so strange, so unreal.

*After more training including eight weeks in the field, Dennis became a fully trained soldier.*

We got called out as a company to help dig out this train that had been lost in the snow. It was a sub-zero winter. We got on a train at Coventry station with our pickaxes and shovels and drove out in blinding snow. Eventually the train stopped because it couldn't go any further, there were great big drifts across the line. The order came, "everybody out!" We had this little quartermaster sergeant and he jumped out and completely vanished into the snow. The snow didn't cover the rest of us, we had our heads above it, but he just disappeared down this hole! You couldn't move your arms, it was a hell of a game; you had to use your elbows and dig yourself up the hole to the top, lie horizontal, roll a bit, tramp the snow down and you could stand up. Everyone except this little sergeant. We felt like leaving him in there.

We marched along the line until we met this enormous wall of snow: "Cut in there as far as you can," we were told. No hot drinks, no hot food, it was just a matter of getting on with it until you dropped. We were saturated and frozen, but at last we dug out the back of the train, the big buffers. We cut along to the door, opened it and there was a train load of passengers inside. They'd been stuck in there for hours. Luckily they'd had the steam heat from the engine to keep warm. We managed to unhook the last carriage with crowbars and get it moving backwards. Eventually we got the train out. It was a hell of a job for us climbing back up into our own train carriages, we were so frozen and wet we could hardly move. When we got back into Coventry they gave us a rum ration, the only time we ever had one. It was lovely and warm, just like fire.

We got called out to different things. Then one day we were issued with tropical kit and thought "bloody hell, we're going out to the Far East"; then we had the lot taken off us and replaced with sub-zero kit. It was all to do with security so nobody could say where we were going. We ended up on board this big troop ship with umpteen decks. We were in the lower echelons somewhere, with no idea where we were headed. We weren't allowed newspapers or the radio; they knew how to addle you, believe me. Eventually we could see the shadow of some land. It got lighter and as we got nearer we could make out these labourers leaning on long-handled shovels. Because of these shovels somebody said, "It's bloody Ireland." They were right. We'd been posted to Ireland.

At one point when we were in Londonderry we got called out to the square. We were told there'd been a blitz on Coventry. All personnel from Coventry or the surrounding areas were to remain in the square and the rest were dismissed. There was a motley collection of us and we were asked if there were any slaters, tilers or bricklayers among us. I wasn't skilled myself, but we were all given free passes to go home. They didn't know what condition our houses were in, or whether our dependants were alive or dead; it was for us to find out.

It was a twenty-four hour journey. I came out of Coventry station and everything was normal until you got out of it. The whole geography of the city was altered. It was just a wrecked mess hidden in a fog of smoke. There were no roads, bricks all over the place, a bit of street would appear and then you'd lose it. I knew the general direction to go in and I can remember clambering over rubble in the direction of Broadgate. Stoney Stanton Road and Foleshill Road had gone. All I had to direct me was a line of poles that had carried the overhead tram wires. They'd all twisted in the heat and that was the only guide. I came to a part where there was very little bomb damage and apart from the roof our house hadn't been touched. Some friends of ours had all been evacuated to a public air raid shelter and there'd been a direct hit on it. They were all wiped out.

We did gas training in Ireland, all to resist a German invasion. Your defence against the lung gases and nerve gases was the Army respirator and the anti-gas cape, which went right down to your boots. Unfortunately you only had to get a tear in that or a leak in your respirator and that was it. They took you through gas-filled chambers in darkness. You'd hear the swish of the tear gas and if you had a leak in your respirator you had to go round the walls, feeling your way until you found the door and then bang like mad until someone opened it. The gas used to make your neck all raw and inflamed where your respirator came round. You could hardly breathe anyway with the equipment on. You also had to fire rifles while you were gassed. The anti-smear cream on your mask was supposed to stop the lens fogging over but you still had a job to line your sights up.

Eventually the Yanks started coming over to Ireland. They were black-skinned from the southern states and they were gentlemen, they really were. They were so good-hearted, even more so than the British troops. If they found out you didn't have a cigarette they'd throw you a carton, not just a packet. That was twenty packs of twenty and they wouldn't take any money for it. They used the same pubs as us, went to the same dances. But then a contingent of white Americans came over and everything changed. Suddenly there was a colour bar. They segregated the pubs and it was blacks over there and whites over here. It was the first time we'd ever come across such a thing. The prices in the white pubs shot right up; that hadn't happened before. They stayed the same in the black pubs. It was terrible because we couldn't really afford the drinks then and just had the occasional dance to go to.

If there was any trouble it was nearly always started by the white Yanks. They'd come into a pub, go straight up to the bar, didn't matter who was there, they'd shoulder their way through and start ordering drinks. The landlord would be all on his own and couldn't keep up so they'd just jump over the bar and start helping themselves, that sort of thing. It was a big shock to us, we wouldn't imagine doing that. Someone would tell the American police and they'd pull up in their

Jeeps and pile in, batons drawn and they'd thrash about whacking people. They'd throw the Yankee squaddies out, literally drag them out and throw them into the Jeeps, chuck them in like a sack of potatoes. It didn't surprise the Americans, they must have been used to that treatment back home I suppose, but it surprised us!

You were told what pubs you could use, what cinemas, right down to what side of the road to walk on. Blacks had to use one side of the road and the whites the other side. If you wanted to cross over you had to go to a special crossing point. The American police were really different to our own. If they told you to do something and you didn't it was a bad do, no messing about.

At one point, when I'd been posted back to England, Montgomery took over, and from day one of his reign as brigadier things changed. We had cross-country runs before breakfast, no matter what the weather was like. We'd go out three weeks to a month at a time on manoeuvres; he really wanted to get us into shape. There was one exercise we did marching at night, full kit, full ammunition, attacking or being attacked. We did 125 miles on that march. Sometimes we had what they called doubling days. As soon as reveille went on the bugle call and your feet touched the ground you had to run on the spot. You had to get dressed running on the spot, you went out on a cross-country run, came back, washed yourself down as best you could and if you were spotted standing still you were on company orders. You could sit when you had your dinner but as

14

soon as your feet touched the floor you had to run on the spot or jog, even when you washed your plate and cup, which was just done in a bucket of water thick as treacle. All day long you were jogging like that until lights out. It nearly killed us but we were fit as fleas.

*After postings in defence at different locations in Britain, Dennis had an accident which led to him leaving the Army.*

I remember getting back to my bed and I can't remember anything else after that. It seemed what had happened is I must have moved an item of kit and my rifle went off. The beds were the height of a man's knee and it just blew my knee off. I can only remember small parts after that, I was drugged you see. The first bit I remember was a voice out of the haze telling me I would be all right, that I was at a casualty clearing station in Dover. God knows how long went by after that, it could have been days and nights, I don't know. They told me they were going to fix a splint on me and that I had a long journey ahead. It ended up with a long rehab and my medical discharge from the Army. My knee is still a terrific trouble even after all these years.

# PART TWO

# IN THE AIR

# Even Better than the Birds

## The Story of Gordon Batt

*Ex-Bablake school boy Gordon Batt was twenty-two when war broke out. A fighter pilot during the Battle of Britain, he flew with 238 Squadron. Gordon's life at this time was spent on alert, waiting for the call to scramble and take to the air.*

I don't think my father ever did get over me joining up, but I think he was proud of me eventually. My brother was the brainy one of the family. They used to get so mad at me at Bablake. Strangely enough I was never any good at school because I did the minimum to get by, but when they said to me at college, "If you don't pass your ground subjects you don't fly, you're out," I started working for the first time ever. My studies at the Technical College started off as night school twice a week plus homework and eventually became day release. You didn't have much time to chase the girls round!

The worst part of a scramble was getting all these false alarms. When the phone went it was most likely change of duties, information, or ask so-and-so to go to headquarters. But then the phone would go and "scramble!" Once you'd got into the aircraft, tucked your wheels up and shut the hood, you felt safe because you'd got something to retaliate with. There would be a rough message to start with: Angels 15 or 20, Southampton or Portsmouth or whatever.

You'd hear the commanding officer shout "Tally Ho!" That meant the enemy had been sighted, although you could see them anyway. I was never really scared, although I'd got my wits about me. I don't think other people were scared either, there were just isolated cases of people who were frightened. You see, when I got into a Hurricane I felt safe, as if I were in my little cocoon, because I could fight back. Not like being on the ground and being bombed. You can't even throw a brick in anger at the devils then.

There was no difference between officers and NCOs in our squadron because we did a lot of fighting from a place called Chilbottom and we were billeted out into the village, so there was very little distinction between us and the officers. In other places like Middle Wallop you might find a blanket across the Nissen hut and the sergeant pilots were on one side and the officers were on the other. Now, in my opinion, that was naughty, but I didn't experience that at all, ever. When I first saw the officers I had a certain opinion of them. At the beginning I thought they were pompous show-offs all dressed up in their hunting red greatcoats, but they acquitted themselves very well in battle and lost a hell of a lot of people, as did we.

My first shooting encounter was over Weymouth. We were six aircraft, that's a flight, and there's two flights in a fighter squadron. We met six Messerschmitts 110s over Chesil beach. They were just probing our defences really, it was where the naval shipyard was, you see. The custom was that we flew the same way, in a line astern. Our flight commander started catching up the enemy tail bloke but their leader was catching *me* up. I thought, "Sod the instruction," and turned round and attacked him head on. I can see myself now hitting him, hitting his wing. I could see the tracer bullets going, spiralling out from the Browning guns. They do something like 800 rounds a minute and it's all over in seconds. In the end he chickened out and flew above me at the last moment. I learnt later that I had a hole in my own wing between the engine and the oil tank.

The nearest I ever got to seeing anyone's face was a Messerschmitt 109 that was attacking one of our Hurricanes. Fortunately I was above him and got on his tail and gave him a burst. Now the armour plating in the 109s came up in a curl above the pilot and he put his head like that and looked so I gave him another burst. He turned on his back then and I did the same. I was waiting for him to come into my sights again but, of course, he didn't come. The 109s were petrol-injected, you see, and could fly very well inverted. We lost power as soon as we were flying on our backs. I had to roll up in the end and he was out of range still flying inverted.

I definitely think I'm a lucky person. I remember once when I got split up from the rest of the squadron.

The bombers had gone and we were left with 110s and 109s. We were isolated there with every bloke for himself. I got involved with two 109s and I was yanking on the stick so hard that I went "schoomp!" and I was spun into the top of a cumulus nimbus cloud. I was spinning so I had to correct my instruments. I came out of the side of this cloud, the ice quickly disappeared and I saw some formation of bombers that must have been split from the main thing. I thought, "Well, I'll have a go at them," and I started to climb up.

Now I was flying in a straight line and it was very seldom that I did that except if I was chasing something. I was stupid. I didn't look and the first thing I knew there were four lines of machine-gun fire coming over my port wing. I went to break one way and thought no and broke the other. The enemy must have been quite close for me to see those four lines of tracer going over but not a bullet hole. Very lucky. It's good fun shooting at people, it's when they start shooting back!

I was actually shot down once but don't ask what hit me because I don't know. You never see the thing that gets you. It felt like a steamroller. When you go "bang", you automatically close your eyes; that's what I did and I hadn't got my goggles on. Well, my eyes were stuck fast with oil. I had to prise them open. There was oil everywhere in the cockpit and a great big dollop hanging off the windscreen. I went through the motions of getting out and opened the hood, but I couldn't smell any burning, so I thought "Right, stick with it". I was streaming engine coolant and no-one else attacked me because I was going straight down. I closed the hood (it was getting damn cold!) and all this oil fell on my lap. I glided north and broke cloud at Selsey Bill. I force-landed with wheels up near a farmhouse in this tiny field of barley. I was pretty well frightened to death. I thought I was going to bash my brains out on the reflector lights. When it stopped I was out and ran along the wing. I can remember that as if it were yesterday. I wake up some nights and think about it and every time I go to sleep again I think about it.

You don't know when you've killed someone. You don't see it. It's not like ordinary warfare. This is why I wanted to be a fighter pilot. First of all your battlefield is clean, there's no blood and gore about and it's all clear in seconds. I didn't particularly hate the Germans but you had to stop them. As an opponent they were ruthless. The Battle of Britain was Hitler's first defeat and it was a combination of radar and us that did it. The Germans had it all their own way before. They'd gone in formations to attack towns in Poland or France and people had no idea where the enemy targets were. With radar we knew before they got there where they were going. The German bombers must have thought, "Where the hell do these people keep coming from?" We would have been lost without radar; there's no doubt in my mind that without it we would have lost the Battle of Britain. Also, except for at the very beginning of the battle we were outnumbered about 4 to 1, but we'd got a lot more targets than they'd got so our lot was pretty easy. They got in one another's way trying to get at us.

There weren't many bombing raids to start with. They weren't organised to such an extent as they were towards the end in August and September time. Prior to that they'd come over in dribs and drabs, half a dozen or a dozen. I think that contributed to me staying alive: I was weaned gently by the time the bigger bomber formations came 400-plus. The bombers would be down below and then behind them and above would be the fighters, the 110s and 109s. They would meet us virtually over the coast.

A wing would go out to meet a big raid like that. A wing was four squadrons, twelve aircraft to each squadron, that's forty-eight fighters. There'd be another wing coming to help us, but we were always the lead squadron because our CO was the most senior. You'd just be thinking, "Here they come again." I'd be weaving at the back. We used to go down on a big formation of bombers and squirt down one line. The Messerschmitt 110s would try to cut us off as we dived; the Spitfires would protect us from them and the 109s would go after the Spitfires.

At the height of the battle we used to get called to London occasionally and we'd patrol over Heathrow. You'd see this mass of twenty, thirty bombers and you could see the ack-ack bursting underneath them. As soon as the CO shouted "Tally Ho!" within seconds all that ack-ack would stop and the controller would say "Right, they're all yours."

Looking for strays was dangerous. I always stayed in the middle of the fight for as long as I could because that was the safest place, as long as you didn't fly in a straight line for too many seconds. The most dangerous thing was sneaking round the edge of a fighter, flying round the outside and being knocked off. If you were on your own, you were outnumbered.

It's no good dreaming when you're a fighter pilot, you've got be able to react quickly. In 1943 someone said to me, "Tell me, you were in the Battle of Britain. You survived it. What can you tell me that will help save my life?" I said, "Look where you've been, not where you're going." In other words, "watch your back."

*During the Battle of Britain Gordon saw a lot of pilots lost. After such a period he admits his survival approach was to make no more friends, even to the point of not knowing the names of some of the men he flew with. His logbook for 1940 shows twenty-five men in his squadron killed.*

I did lose one very good friend. He'd been with me from the time the Squadron was formed at Tangmere. He shouted, "Look out, Gordon!" but he'd already been hit himself. Fortunately I hadn't been billeted with him so that made it a bit easier for me.

You mixed with people but you didn't get too friendly. I had to consciously stop making friends, but it didn't have any lasting effect on me. The one thing that's difficult for you to understand is that OK, it was very dangerous and you could lose your life, but you didn't even think about that. Your life was pretty full from dawn to dusk. You made arrangements to go out in the evening, decided which pub had got beer and sort of headed that way, but you never assumed you weren't coming back.

When I remember those times I think I was extremely lucky to fly. It's even better than birds, because the birds can't loop the loop and slow roll. No, I wouldn't have missed my flying for anything. Marvellous. When you see this cumulus nimbus sprouting up on a summer's day you notice all the bottoms of the cloud; to fly around those and chop a bit off, go in and out, it's marvellous. It gives me a good feeling when I look back.

# They Lived for the Day

## The Story of Reg Farmer

Reg Farmer was born four days before the start of the First World War. He had started up his own printing business in Hill Street before joining the RAF in July 1940. Among other duties he wrote the squadron lettering on Spitfires in his role as aircraftsman 2nd class: "really the lowest form of life!" Reg was part of the ground crew at Biggin Hill for three months during the Battle of Britain where he served with 92 Squadron, one of the famous Spitfire outfits.

When we arrived the place had been completely blitzed: the hangars, workshops, hospitals and billets were absolutely flattened. It was my first sight of bomb devastation and it was quite a shock. One morning, I remember, the post came in and on this occasion it was me who had to go over and fetch the mailbag. I picked it up and I was on my way back, when all of a sudden I heard one of these raiders come in and I saw this guy; he came out of the low cloud and he was banging away with his machine-gun. Fortunately there was a ditch alongside the road so I dived in there and I pulled the mailbag on top of me! Anyhow, of course, he was gone in a minute. It was so quick.

There were chaps from all over the world at Biggin Hill. We had an American on the Squadron before the Americans came into the war. We had a Frenchman, a Pole, a New Zealander, a Canadian; he was shot down early on. He'd been in the Canadian mounted police and whenever he flew he would wear his red coat. There was quite a gulf between the lower ranks and the officers. There was no social mixture. We could go down to the pub at night and there might be some sergeant pilots in the same bar, but you wouldn't usually see an officer in there, they'd drink somewhere else. You'd always say "sir" to an officer, you didn't bother with a sergeant. They were all right, don't get me wrong, because there's no men in this world I have ever admired more than the pilots because, you imagine, they never knew if the next sortie they went on would be their last. Some of them were a wild sort of bunch, but on the other hand you could understand it. They lived for the day and that's all they could do because they never knew when their time was coming.

You got so used to death. In a way you kind of had to blank it off. Everything was happening so instantly, you were literally hardened to it. Just to give you one instance: a friend of mine named Bunningham was with me down on dispersal one day when we had about four new pilots come in. We looked at these sergeant pilots and Bunny said, "There's old so-and-so over there." He went over to him and it was a chappy we both knew. I was quite pally with him, he came from Nuneaton. I said hello and that sort of thing. Well, there was a scramble and for some reason this new pilot took a plane up and that was it. He didn't come back. He wasn't shot down. We understood that at 20,000ft his oxygen had run out and, of course, you pass out. So he wasn't on the squadron more than half an hour.

When a pilot was killed we had to form a guard of honour. I remember on one particular occasion there was a policeman from Bromley, the nearest town to Biggin Hill. He'd got his first kill in the afternoon and he said, "When I come down again I'll get you to put my coat of arms on my Mae West in a cross beer bottle sort of thing." So I said "OK" and he went up and of course he didn't come back, he was shot down. The next thing I had to do with five others was to carry his coffin to the local cemetery for his funeral.

I remember one day which had been a busy one. The Squadron was in action again. We were waiting for their return when we heard an aeroplane approaching. This single Spitfire came out of the cloud. It was one of our kites, "G" for George. It flew slowly right across our dispersal with its wheels still up. We thought it was going to make another circuit before perhaps making an emergency belly landing but nothing happened. It disappeared into the sky. Well, the rest of the Squadron returned but not "G" for George. Nothing was heard of it the next day or the one after and we nearly forgot about it. A few weeks later it was found. It had landed in the top of some high trees in the wood.

When the recovery team reached the Spitfire with ladders they only found one hole in the side of the cockpit canopy where a cannon shell had entered and a hole in the other side where it had left. Half the pilot's head was gone. It must have killed him instantly: his hand was still on the control column. He'd guided his Spitfire back to base miles away from where he'd met his death. He was a flight lieutenant, a New Zealander, one of The Few who gave their lives in that crucial battle.

*In November 1940 Reg was posted to RAF Locking near Weston-super-Mare for flight mechanic training. He was given immediate leave when Coventry was blitzed. He hitch-hiked home to find his house destroyed.*

One thing I shall never forget is standing on a pile of bricks that had been my home. Sometimes I found familiar items lying torn and scattered around me. It's difficult for you to imagine how we felt about things because so much was happening that you kind of got hardened. You were philosophical about it. With the bombing of Coventry, the only thing I could be glad about was the fact that my parents were all right. Although our home had gone we still thought, "Well, that's it." It had happened to thousands of other people too.

The majority of the present generation haven't got any real conception of what it was like. I mean I know you've got all these films, but until you actually experience these things you just don't know. You grew to accept everything, and apart from what was happening to you and what was happening to the country as a whole or to the lads overseas, you were just a small part of the big thing and you had to accept everything because there was literally nothing you could do about it. You couldn't question it.

I don't think the majority of people ever thought we were going to lose the war but on the other hand we couldn't see how we could possibly win. Before the Americans came in I couldn't see any hope. I always contend that the Battle of Britain was the most important battle of the war. We were expecting an invasion every day; they reckoned there were bodies washed up on the beach, there were all sorts of rumours. You can't reproduce the feeling that was there.

# That's the Day I Should Have Died

## The Story of Alan Hartley

Alan Hartley joined the RAF at eighteen and served as a mechanic from 1943 in 271 Squadron. From his airfield at Down Ampney he saw the planes leave to supply troops for D-Day and Arnhem.

I actually volunteered for the RAF as an air gunner at seventeen and a half, but failed the medical because of a perforated eardrum. When I received my National Service call-up papers I had to go back to Sibree Hall, but this time the doctor was my own GP and he knew how keen I was to get into the RAF. He held a watch to my deaf ear and said, "Can you hear that?" I said yes without blinking and he passed me through. In July 1943 I reported to Padgate near Warrington and the day after I joined Mussolini packed in.

I ended up at a place called Down Ampney in Gloucestershire along with the thirty men I'd trained with. It was very primitive; Nissen huts, thirty to a hut, uncovered concrete floor. The camp wasn't finished and towards the end of spring the mud started to dry and turned to dust and you got dirt on everything. You grew up quickly, but paradoxically you used to have pillow fights in your billets which you wouldn't have done at home. I think the services gave us an extension of our youth.

We arrived at the very end of February and flying into Down Ampney with us was Billy, the squadron dog, a terrier that had been found abandoned on a French airfield. He'd started off with the squadron in Doncaster and at the camp there he used to walk up the road, wait at the bus stop and catch the bus into town. He'd go round all the pubs where he knew airmen were and he'd get a saucer of beer and a packet of crisps in each, then he'd go back to the bus stop, hop on the bus and the driver would let him off back at camp.

That dog could ride a bike. He never liked to walk the 2 miles round dispersal at Down Ampney and if an airman went by on a bike he'd stop and say "Come on, Billy" and Billy would jump up, front paws on the handle bar. He lost all his teeth fetching stones for airmen. He always had to be first in the queue at the NAAFI, and if he wasn't he'd nip your ankles with his gums. Sometimes when we were sitting around playing cards or whatever, you'd see Billy sitting there with a piece of cake between his ears. As soon as someone said "Right, Billy!" he'd flick his head back and catch the cake. A worrying thing happened though. Sometimes Billy used to go up in the planes and fly with the crew. One day he got on an aircraft heading for Brussels and when the plane came back one of the lads said,

"There's no sign of Billy. He's gone. Lost at Brussels."
We were all very sad to lose the squadron dog like that.
Ten days later trotting up the camp came Billy, pristine
white and with a big pink bow tied round his neck. We
never did find out what he'd been up to in those
missing days. Probably some Belgian girl had cleaned
him up for us.

After arriving at Down Ampney we spent the next
few months training on Dakota engines. Everything was
being practised in camp: parachute and supplies
dropping, glider towing, air ambulance, bringing back
casualties. It was all leading up to D-Day. Just before 6
June they sealed off all the camp's phone boxes and all
the mail had to be opened for the officers to read. The
morning these orders came out I'd just got my leave
pass for seven days. I knew the cook and managed to
get my hands on some butter, some sugar, some bacon
and a hare that we'd shot. I'd just made my way out of
camp and was off down the road when I was spotted by
some red caps.

"Airman, where do you think you're going?"

"I'm going home," I said.

"The camp's sealed. Get back." So I lost my seven
days' leave, but luckily they didn't look in my bag. If
they'd seen the sugar, butter and bacon I could have
been court-martialled for stealing rations.

We were given an order thirty-six hours before
D-Day to paint all the Dakotas with black and white
stripes so our Navy could spot them and protect them.
Every spare hand got stuck in. Billy was running
between the planes all excited at the activity. People

34

would give him a swipe with their brush, "Go on now, Billy, out the way." You've never seen a dog change so much from black to white back to black again.

D-Day morning at about six thirty we were down at the dispersal when one mechanic said, "Ooh, look at this lot", and marching towards us were this group of paratroopers all with a Cherokee haircut: heads shaved with just a V left. They had warpaint on their faces and meat cleavers in their belts. We thought it was a bit of bull with the meat cleavers. Anyway they clambered aboard the Dakotas and we saw them off. We all thought the same thing; glad they were going that way and not coming this way. They were the Canadians and they looked a fearsome lot.

When the aircraft were coming back in from D-Day we would be notified by the tannoy system. All round camp we had big loudspeakers on poles and they would tell us, "Casualty aircraft coming in. All available aircrew report to the apron." The apron was the hard standing area. Whatever we were doing at the time, cup of tea in the NAAFI, anything at all, we'd get straight down there. There would be one air ambulance nurse on each Dakota. They were only about eighteen or nineteen years old and they got just 8d a day, would you believe. It wasn't unusual for a man who had been wounded at D-Day to be back being operated on at Down Ampney in three hours. We'd help the stretchers on to the ambulance and sometimes we travelled in the ambulance with them.

One day they brought a German POW back. He'd got his socks on but no boots. We took him to the hospital where he got cleaned up, washed and shaved. He spoke very good English and he told us he'd lain on the beach for four days pretending to be dead. A Frenchman had come and taken his boots. I'm telling you the truth when I say the reason he was pretending to be dead was that he'd seen the Canadian paratroopers, the ones with the shaved heads, going round the beach cutting off German heads with their meat cleavers.

When the wounded came in they were marked either as stretcher cases, walking wounded or SIW, "self-inflicted wound". I never saw any of those, they did happen but were very rare. The lads that came back had burn marks; they were yellow, drained of blood, all bandaged up by the nurse. One poor bloke was flown back to our base five or six days after D-Day. His Jeep had hit a mine and tipped over, trapping him underneath; the petrol tank exploded and he was very badly injured. The aircraft he came back in smelt terrible for days. It was the smell of burnt flesh. We talked about it in the NAAFI. It was awful.

I never lost anybody close. As a mechanic you're not really at the sharp end. I saw a few tragedies at Down Ampney though. Our flight sergeant was coming back on his bike and this Dakota stopped and asked him if he wanted a bit of a joyride. They were practising close formation flying for when they dropped the paratroopers on D-Day. He put his bike on board and went up with them. There was an accident in the air and they were all killed.

There were a few sad incidents with paratroopers as well. On one occasion one of them jumped and got caught up in the tail wing of the Dakota. They couldn't get him back in, his face was turning black and blue with bruising. They got another plane to escort the Dakota over the sea where he was dropped. A motor boat was waiting to pick him up, but it was too late for him and he died on the way to hospital. I saw another tragedy when one of our paratroopers was suspended between his bag rope and his parachute shrouds high up in a tree. He was quite happy, we were shouting up to him, teasing him. A fireman climbed up to him on his ladder, but instead of cutting the rope he pressed the release button on the parachute. The whole harness dropped and the weight of the paratrooper came down on the top of the ladder which buckled and crashed to the ground. The fireman landed on top of the paratrooper and he was killed outright. One minute he had been laughing and joking with us and the next he was dead.

We would go up in the Dakotas if we got the chance. There are four aircrew: a pilot, a second pilot, a navigator and a wireless operator. We had a mechanic for the airframe and a mechanic for the engines, so it was a team of six, and over the months of training you got to know each other very well, built up a good rapport. You would fly with them whenever you could, and they were pleased if the mechanic flew because it meant the engines were good and everything was tight. Flying in a Dakota was like flying in a big fat petrol tank. There were two 1,800hp engines and we flew at

150mph, doors open with the slipstream coming in: it was very noisy and cold.

The closest I ever came to danger was in a Dakota. I went for a ride over Cheltenham with my mate Dick one day. Near the door where the paratroopers used to jump the floor was quite slippery under Army boots, so they used to tape down this piece of coconut matting. On my joyride I was lying on this mat with my head out the door. Suddenly I realised that the rigger had cleaned the plane but he hadn't taped down the coconut matting and I could feel it slipping. The plane started to bank over Cheltenham and I could feel myself sliding out the door. My mate Dick saw what was happening, dived down and dragged me back in. I was rather white-faced after that.

My pilot, Len Wilson, took a glider to Arnhem. When he came back I asked him what it was like. "Absolutely fantastic," he said, "You could see all the different parachutes, all different colours, medical, supplies, ammunition, heavy ammunition, rifles, all the gliders. Absolutely wonderful."

So I said, "Right, tomorrow morning I'm going over for a joyride, have a look at the battle." I was all set to go the next day and then down came Len. "I'm sorry, Alan," he said, "There's another aircraft with a trimming fault and I'm senior pilot so I've got to take that one. I've had a word with the chap who's taking our aeroplane and he's agreed to take you." This chap came down. He was a peacetime officer with a cheese-cutter cap and gloves. You had to be all "yes sir! yes sir!" saluting all the time and nobody liked him. I made an excuse and I didn't go. That decision saved my life.

When our lads came in the Germans were waiting for them and just knocked them out of the sky. We lost eleven or twelve aircraft including the one I would have gone in and the one Len took up. As he pulled away from the dropping zones he got hit by an anti-aircraft gun near the woods at the edge of Arnhem. He tried to crash his aircraft on to this gun to make sure it didn't shoot anyone else, but as he got close he must have died because he ended up flying to the right, missed the gun and finished up hitting a tree in the garden behind these houses. They were all killed except for the wireless operator who had managed to parachute out; he was taken prisoner of war, but got home in the end.

The Dakotas taking supplies over to Arnhem were told to fly in a straight line for two minutes at 120mph, 500ft above the ground, because they were short of parachutes and the unbreakable supplies had to be dropped freefall from wickerwork panniers. They had no fighter escort, no guns to fire back and flew in broad daylight. They were flying so low they even had machine-guns and rifles shooting at them. When those planes came back you could see the damage. There were gliders with broken wings, Dakotas smoking with big holes in the wings, small holes in the fuselage. They did this for four days in a row. You could see the strain on the airmen. Lots of them were family men. We were desperately sorry for them when they went up, worrying about how they would get on. To see the lads coming down with white faces knowing they had to go back again, I have the utmost respect for them. They had to go in to get the supplies to the 10,000 men on the floor. We lost about seventeen planes and their aircrew at Arnhem. In my opinion, those four days supplying the troops at Arnhem saw some of the bravest flying in the war.

March 1945, we suddenly got an order from Down Ampney that thirty of us mechanics were to be at the mess at half past four. I went down with all my small kit, shaving gear, what have you, and we were sent somewhere on the east coast. We arrived at night time and the flying bombs were coming over. You could hear them looking for us.

On 24 March at half past six in the morning we filled our aircraft up with petrol, inspected them and then they took the gliders up: thirty Dakotas taking thirty gliders, one went up every minute and a half. I stood and watched. There were Lancasters as far as the eye could see, left, right, centre, all different heights and masses of other planes: Halifaxes, Stirlings, Mosquitoes, Spitfires, Thunderbolts, Hurricanes, all going east. The whole ground shook with the noise of the engines. Then way up in the perfect blue sky was an orange flare and circling it were the Fortresses. These Fortresses came from every angle until they had formed a box of twelve and then that would fly off and another Fortress would drop a flare and another box would build up. It was the most wonderful, awe inspiring sight I've ever seen in my life.

About twenty-five years ago I visited where Len's plane came down at Arnhem and got to know the people who lived there. The tree is still standing and you can see where the trunk was sheered off by the wing and these little branches growing out.

The crew were buried in the garden behind the houses. The bodies were moved to the airborne cemetery later and buried in the same line formation as they had been in the garden. I go back to Arnhem every year to the house where the tree stands. They were going to widen the road once and cut the tree down and the whole neighbourhood got together, said the spot where the Dakota crashed was a historic one and saved the tree. So it's called "Alan's Tree" now and it's protected. It should be called "Len's Tree" because Len was the skipper, but they call it after me. I went over this year and they told me that a fortnight earlier there'd been a machine cutting the tree. My host had run out. "You can't touch that tree, it's protected." This chap said, "Oh, I know, it's Alan's Tree, but it's not very well so I'm pruning it to give it a better chance of health." My Dutch host gave me a branch off the tree, her husband drilled it and I put candles in it. So that's the day I should have died: 19 September 1944.

# Ordinary Chaps with a Job To Do

## The Story of Bob Barley

Bob Barley was living in Poplar Road, Earlsdon, and working as a sign-writer when he joined the RAF in 1941. Posted to Canada aged nineteen, Bob trained to fly in Tiger Moths. As he says himself, he came unstuck later in his training flying twin-engine planes and changed track to become an air gunner.

I've always been interested in aircraft and anything mechanical. We used to go on our bikes and cycle down to the airfields at Brize Norton and Upper Hayford in Oxford. I was in the Home Guard as soon as war broke out and when the time came I went down to Sibree Hall and joined up as an air gunner. I had the idea that I'd like to get in the Air Force and it was best to volunteer: if you left it until you were called up you might find yourself in the Army regardless. There was a medical, you had to answer questions. They had a lot of models of planes for aircraft recognition and you had to tell them what they were. I did quite well at that and they could see I was interested and said to me "Why not go for pilot?" So I did.

*After some initial training in England Bob was posted overseas.*

We collected our flying kit, goggles and stuff, got on the train and went up to Gourock on the Clyde. We had a rough idea we were being sent to Canada because that was one of the main training places. It was a pretty ancient boat that we sailed on. All the crew were American and there were a lot of American soldiers on board travelling here and there. The journey took three weeks. Too long! I was sick all the way. We were down in the hold, below the waterline. It was a bit claustrophobic, they really stacked them in. I could reach out from my bunk and touch about sixteen men, it was that tight. We got good grub from the Americans though, but then again it was stuff we weren't used to, cabbage and pineapple for pudding. They served up chops covered in sugar one day; they loved sugar with everything.

While we were on board we used to sing, "There'll Always be an England" and the American men used to sing "There'll always be an England while there's a USA!" I quite liked most of them though. What struck me was that they were either all discipline or no discipline. Some of our people went to train in America and the discipline was out of this world. But the other side of it, you got chaps that just never seemed to bother, they nattered away to officers calling them "Bill" and "Joe".

We landed at Halifax and the Canadians were very good; the women came along with chocolate bars and fruit. I went to the Canadian prairies on the initial pilots' training and there was just miles and miles of nothing, just corn and wheat waving in the wind. My first solo flight was on 23 April 1942. It was a dream come true. After you've finished you go round and tell your friends that you've soloed. You don't do very much really; the main thing is to take off, do a circuit, come round and land and then your instructor would say, "That's good enough, so round again."

It's a terrific buzz to fly when you're on your own, it really is. You're nervous at the start but once you get the feel of the thing it's just very elating. It was a great experience for me and for most of the chaps, I think. I trained for aerobatics too. You'd gain altitude, do the spin, pick the power up and gradually stall the aircraft and it sort of drops. When it drops you put left or right rudder on, the aircraft immediately flicks down and you have to put full power on and straighten out. It was a bit of a thrill. We didn't get nervous beforehand, you must remember we were young lads, young and daft.

The type of flying you ended up with, fighter pilot or whatever, depended partly on your temperament. Everybody wanted to be a Spitfire pilot really! They decided I was a steady sort of bloke, but I wasn't really disappointed because I thought it was more my type of thing, flying straight and level. I came unstuck though; I didn't manage the twin-engine aircraft and I was sent to southern Ontario where I trained as an air gunner. I did well on that and ended up as an instructor for eighteen months. I trained Americans, Canadians, Australians. It wasn't what I wanted — I wanted to get home. I used to write to my mum every week, about fourteen pages! Letters were very important to us then.

We came back from Canada on a French passenger liner, so it was a bit more civilised. If you had a cabin one chap would be on the table, one sleeping underneath and another slung in a hammock above the table. If you were on top and you fell out, you'd fall on the bloke below.

*After leaving Canada Bob was posted to Loch Erne in Northern Ireland for operational training and on to Sullom Voe in the Shetlands where he flew with 210 Squadron until the end of the war.*

I was always at sea. We escorted convoys, mostly those coming down from Iceland. Air gunners were in the tail of the aircraft, the middle or the nose. I went out on flying boats called Catalinas and my job was to fire the guns. Sighting was quite a job. You'd be moving up and down in the air and your target would be moving around and circling, so it was very different to sighting a target on land.

Our main job was looking out for submarines. We'd work with other squadrons going on information from intelligence who might say, for example, "There's three U-boats in such and such an area" and we'd then fly over a block of ocean, each plane covering a different area. You'd patrol your patch, dropping sonar buoys down into the sea and listening for the U-boat. An average flight would be about sixteen hours, the longest trip we did was up to the north of Norway. The squadron sank eight German U-boats during the war, four of those at the end, as we'd got better radar then.

There were nine of us in the Catalina and you'd always be with the same men. I can honestly say we weren't scared when we went out, we were always too busy. There was so much to do, especially at the beginning of a trip. I'd go up in the front gun turret, set up the guns, fire them, test them and spend an hour there. An hour was as long as you'd want to be there if you were up in the Arctic because the front was open and it was freezing! You couldn't stand the cold for too long. You'd have all your flying gear on, three roll-neck sweaters and what we called subsocks, the type worn by submariners, which went right up to your thighs, but it was still freezing.

We'd change round every hour: I'd go from the front turret to the guns in the blisters, that's the ones either side of the aircraft; the second engineer would go on the front guns and somebody would be on rest. We called it rest, but that's when you would be really busy because people would say, "How about a cup of tea? How about getting the meals going?" Generally when I came out of the front to go to the back turret, the wireless operator and the engineer would be peeling spuds. There were two Primus stoves. We'd have two meals, we had coffee in a bottle, tea and something like Oxo, so you could have a hot drink, which you really needed. I remember one of our barmy New Zealanders had the Primus stoves sitting on the tanks of ammunition once! When a Primus stove doesn't light up properly you get all these big flames, and there they were, perched on top of the ammunition.

A crew is a unit and we'd go everywhere together, even on leave. With friends you were always thinking you might not see them at breakfast the following morning. During my time with 210 Squadron we lost four aircraft and two were badly damaged but managed to get back. That wasn't bad compared to others: the Catalina was the safest aircraft to fly in during the war. I did lose some friends. I lost some when I was training as a pilot. It would be mentioned, but we didn't make a big thing of it. It made you think a bit, but you just carried on. I always feel a bit sad on Remembrance Day. I had an easy war compared to such a lot of people. We were all ordinary chaps and it was a job we had to do.

# PART THREE

# AT SEA

# You Can Say Goodbye when it's Forty Below

## The Story of Les Lengden

Les Lengden was an aircraft fitter in his native Coventry and had been in the Home Guard at Baginton before he volunteered for the Royal Navy in 1941 at the age of twenty-two. Two of Les's five years' service were spent in the engine room of the destroyer HMS *Oakley* where he sailed the coast of North Africa, into the Arctic and as far as Russian waters.

I knew I would eventually get called up so I volunteered for the Royal Navy. I've always liked the sea. I finished up going down to Warwick Row for the medical, finally got in about November and went straight to Portsmouth. I went in as a petty officer because I'd already got a trade as a fitter. It wasn't too bad. It was a bit of a shock in the sense of training, discipline, marching up and down and night duties. It was different to what I was used to!

We were lucky because there were five of us in a nice little mess and our conditions were good. We had a mess man who cooked our meals. You had all the water you wanted, but you washed in sea water, not very nice. You washed your blankets in sea water too, just trampled them. I brought those home and they never did get soft, they stayed hard; they were horrible.

You had to get permission from the captain to grow a beard. A lot of the lads put in to grow one when we were going up to the Arctic from Aberdeen and you can't shave it off until you leave for home. We were out there two or three months and you should have seen some of them . . . little bits of hair growing here, little bits there. There was one chap and his beard came out like a packet of Players. When we came back, you requested to shave off.

"Permission to shave off, sir!"

"And I should ruddy well think so!"

The worst part was that right next to our engine room hatch was what they call the pom-pom, a gun that fires shells. The noise of that was terrible, like being in a dustbin with somebody banging the top. It was rough at times; you wouldn't be able to sleep, you couldn't stand up because of the sea. We needed an engineer at one time and we had a chap come off a big battleship, and he only lasted a week, the poor devil. He was all over the place and sick all the time because that's a different motion you see on a battleship.

Funnily enough the west coast of England was the worst bit of sailing I ever did. There was one lad of about eighteen who got washed out of the gun turret by the sea. Lucky for him we weren't in action so we could go astern. The bosun went over on a line and we picked him up out of the sea. He was in the sick bay for a couple of days. Well, he had to go up before the skipper and he got a fortnight's stoppage of leave for leaving the ship without permission! He should have been more careful, he shouldn't have been washed out you see. That's the idea. That's discipline.

If you got torpedoed you could say goodbye, no chance. You've got steam at 750lb pressure, you can't even see that when it comes out: if it hits you you've had it altogether. I came off watch one afternoon and I was standing in midships looking out. The sea was pretty flat and I heard a watchman shout "Torpedo!" and this torpedo came and went straight underneath where I was standing. Luckily it was set too deep, so it didn't do anything. Well, I laughed, but the next minute you realise what might have happened and it quite upsets you. I was as white as a sheet when I went below. Our ship was lucky, never hit and nobody killed. Out of nine Hunt-class destroyers, we lost seven over the war, I believe. We'd talk about it. Could have been us. We could have been in the water, that's the point.

I was fortunate in the sense of being below; I didn't see too much of people getting killed, thank goodness. To see ships burning when you come up: that's a sad thing. I was in a situation up in the Arctic once. Four of us Hunt-class destroyers went to pick up a tugboat which was towing an R-class destroyer that had been torpedoed. There were thirty men on it and we were told that if the weather got bad it would go. Well, it did go. All these fellows were prepared with their gear on, but you've got to imagine, it was forty below. The four of us destroyers got round so that the searchlights were right on it and the men got off on the Carley floats and all sorts of things. I came up from below and tried to help. It was difficult, everyone was so frozen. We'd got the nets down hanging over the side for the men to climb up on. We got two out, one a lad of about eighteen. They were frozen but they were fighting for their lives, they got the strength from somewhere. The rest of the ships got some others out. We only saved seventeen out of that lot, the rest were frozen stiff on the Carley float. When you go in the sea without any gear on, you can say goodbye when it's forty below. They were geared up, got everything on but they still couldn't make it. I can hear them now and again; it sticks in your mind.

We wondered what was going on at home, but when you're on board ship sometimes you get that busy it keeps your mind off things. When you weren't busy you were trying to get some sleep. I mean I've slept against a diesel on some occasions because I was that busy. You'd have four hours on, four hours off, then you'd have dawn action stations, at four or five o'clock and the next one would be in the evening. Whatever happened to us was in between. Dawn or evening is the time a submarine or aircraft could attack because it's not very light. At action stations everyone would stand at their posts. You'd go to your spots, us engineers would be by the generators or down below waiting — be prepared you see.

At one action stations some torpedo bombers attacked us. We were down below and we were awake for nearly twenty-four hours before we got to sleep again. That was the incident when we got these two Italian airmen. We shot one down, the other got away and then we picked the two of them up. I'd come off watch and there they were looking very sad for themselves, very miserable. We gave them a cup of tea, took them back and a fortnight later they were on our side! That's the silly part of war.

We didn't get much leave, but I remember once I walked up our yard and all my mother said was that I was just in time to take the blackout down. I realise now she didn't know what to say to me. I used to go to the Cottage in Earlsdon. People treated you well on leave, they'd want to know what was going on. They went out of their way when they knew I was coming. They'd gather all their rations together and I wouldn't realise what they'd sacrificed.

*Les had met Jean in July 1942, a few months before he joined up.*

When he came home on leave he used to come to the Cheyne and meet me. There were three friends, me and two other girls. I was engaged to a sailor, one was engaged to an airman and one to a soldier, and all three used to be sitting outside to meet us.

It was a strange affair really. I only knew him July to November and he came home on leave in January the following year and he said "We'll get engaged and we'll get married on my next leave". Well, I never saw him again for two years. He came home on the Monday in the January of 1945 and the following Tuesday we got married. I didn't really know him. We've been married sixty years now.

I got machine-gunned near the Alvis! Me and my friend had been home for lunch and were going back to work through the Cheyne Garden. It had been snowing and everything was white. There was this one plane and he was on his way home. He'd bombed the Standard Motor Company and he got a medal for it. Anyway, I guess he spotted us: we'd stand out in the snow, two girls and nobody else around. He was pretty low and firing at us. We just threw ourselves into a hedge and hoped he'd miss us. It was frightening, but at that age we thought it was hilarious. You think, "Ooh! I've been machine-gunned!" Thinking about it now I'd have a fit.

*At the end of the war Les took part in the occupation of Kiel in Germany.*

Before we went for the occupation we had a briefing telling us what the Germans were like. Six foot tall and broad like this, that's what they taught us. I think they wanted to frighten us, make sure we'd stand up, realise what we were up against. But we weren't up against anything. It was just like coming here and meeting people in the streets.

We travelled three or four days in these lorries, all scruffy and dirty, and when we got to Kiel there were all these German people, little tiny people really, overalls on, and they couldn't help us enough getting stuff off the wagon. This young soldier lad gave a German his rifle to carry! It was so funny. I was the only Coventry man out of about 250, all tradesmen. When you were celebrating VE Day I was travelling down there.

I had a map of Kiel and we had to go round to see if there was anything left of the factories. It was really flattened, the riverside was 7 miles of absolute chaos. The people themselves were in a pathetic way. They were people just the same as us. You've got to remember the Nazis and the Germans are different altogether.

I went to a house one day. Their places were worse than ours, the conditions and the food and everything. I'll always remember, I went up the stairs and I had a .45 on me; I knocked on the door and this poor old lady put her arm up to defend herself and I said "No! No!" It was very tough for them.

All the German destroyers were brought into Kiel. When I was there one of these destroyers started to go over. The Royal Marines took the German engineer and were going to shoot him the next day for destroying the ship. They sent for me and I went down to his cell and saw him. I can picture him now: he was a man of about forty-five or so. I went back to his ship and he explained to me, and I knew as an engineer, what had happened. You have to trim your ship by its water tanks to keep it upright. When they got the Germans off at Kiel they whipped him off too without giving him time to resettle the ship. It wasn't his fault the destroyer was listing. Anyway, I managed to save him.

War made a man of me because I was a nervous chap in a way. You had to live up to it or go down. I used to be a Methodist, but I'm afraid I'm not very religious at all now. It was the war that did that because I came across so many religions and thought about what was actually going on.

We used to go to the Memorial Park on Remembrance Day, but we can't stand any more and they only have seats for the councillors. So we go to the end of the road here and watch the parade go by. It's very emotional, I feel full up. I count myself as fortunate, a lot of us didn't make it back. I remember, on the coast of North Africa, seeing a skull with a tin hat on — that was one of our blokes. Whoever takes part in it, war is a sad thing.

# It's Got To Be the Navy

## The Story of Reg Walker

Although Reg Walker had tried to volunteer for the Navy at sixteen, he had to wait until just after his seventeenth birthday in 1943 to join up successfully. After completing his training Reg began his service as signalman on the Pretoria Castle, an auxiliary aircraft carrier.

I think what really started it was a family holiday in the Isle of Man. I was absolutely fascinated with the ships, I couldn't get over them. At the time I left school there was one ship in particular, HMS *Hood*, and I saw pictures of it: sailors astride guns, hats raised in the air, grins on their faces and I thought "It's got to be the Navy". I went to volunteer and said I was seventeen, which I wasn't. They found out I was only sixteen and told me to come back after my birthday. My mum and dad couldn't understand why I was upset when I couldn't get in.

When I finished my training I had the choice of three different divisions to join: the Devonport division, the Portsmouth division or Chatham division. Well, my brother was at Felixstowe on motor torpedo boats, so I thought if I went to Chatham I'd have a good chance of meeting up with him. In the event I didn't, and I've wondered ever since: if I'd have chosen one of the other two would I have been here now? My cousin and a school friend, who lived a few doors away in Stanley Road, both joined up in 1944 and served on the same ship together. It was torpedoed that same year; my friend died and my cousin survived. It was all very much a lottery.

When I joined the *Pretoria Castle*, it was an aircraft carrier. We would carry out trials for every new innovation that was dreamed up and also train airmen to take off and land. They would be transferred to other ships once they'd passed out. Planes would take off as soon as you got into the Clyde Estuary. They'd do a few circles and then come back in to land. There's a hook at the back of the aircraft which drops down, catches the arrester wires and pulls the plane to a halt. Often, with the inexperience, they would miss these wires and crash into the barrier or even hop over it. We were often losing aircraft, planes going over into the sea or something. On one occasion we had a Swordfish aircraft that missed the arrest wires, hopped over the barriers and crashed into the bridge. The propeller shattered and bits of it flew all over. Everybody, officers or whatever, threw themselves to the floor. Accidents like that happened quite frequently, but invariably the pilots were rescued. We did lose one in the night time. We were in the Firth of Clyde. He went over the top into the water and we never found him. You just had to accept it when things like that happened. It was bad luck.

The *Pretoria Castle* had been a liner before, and so our conditions were quite luxurious compared with normal warships. On a purpose-built warship toilets never had doors or anything, which we did. We slept in hammocks in a large space called the forecastle. Your mess tables were all along the bulkhead towards the centre of the ship and your hammocks were slung over the top. You were often asleep when people were having a meal down below.

With an aircraft carrier you're pitching and rolling at the same time. I was only ever seasick once. In rough seas you'd still be up there doing your duties if you were on watch. You'd be wearing maybe a duffel coat and you'd quite often get soaking wet. I could be about 70ft up and still see green seas coming over sometimes. It wasn't very pleasant, but with all these things you came to accept it and it was part of your life. Mind you, if your relief was a couple of minutes late the air would be quite blue!

At harbour in Greenock we saw a load of ships come in with the GIs. One or two were skippered by film stars. George Montgomery was skipper of a destroyer; we couldn't see him but we knew he was there. I spoke to a few Americans when I was on leave because you'd find them all over town. There wasn't any animosity towards them, why should there be? They were there for the common good, a common cause.

I remember once when we were anchored off the Isle of Man and we'd gone ashore. We only had 14s a week, but we were buying whiskies because they were quite cheap. I went to a dance and all of a sudden the room spun round and I just crawled under a bench. I was carried to what they called a liberty boat, like a fishing boat, to take us to the ship. I had ropes attached round me and I was hauled up, because of the danger. I probably would have been killed trying to climb up the ladder in my state. I had the indignity of photographs being taken because the ship's photographer was on board.

Whenever there were any U-boats around, we were escorted into harbour because we were considered too valuable. Before the war we used to get a lot of cowboy films. In those days the good guys always wore a white hat and the bad guy wore a black hat. I didn't really know much, the Germans were just the guys in the black hats to us. You won't get a serviceman with anything bad to say about a German serviceman, particularly in the Navy, because in the Navy you only have one enemy and that's the sea.

We were in port when news came that the war was over. I was in my hammock. I heard someone say "He doesn't know yet" and I didn't even put my head up or anything. I felt sort of mixed emotions, I suppose. Obviously, there were many around who would have leapt high into the air, but I was never in the front line stuck well into danger.

At the end of the war I was posted to Germany to join a motor launch. Before I went I had to go to Sheerness for the small arms drills. We had to learn how to use a revolver and something like a tommy-gun. When we got to Germany we were just walking around among Germans as you would in town here, it was no problem. When we had to go to a port in the Russian area, every Russian soldier we saw wore their medals, big medals, and every one was armed with a rifle and a gun in the holster. We found exactly the same thing with the Americans further down.

We weren't supposed to fraternise with the Germans in any way at the time, no contact at all, but I did meet up with a family. The father worked in the dockyard, he was getting on a bit. We could buy anything we wanted, beer or fancy cakes, and I used to take these up to them. They hadn't seen anything like it for a long time.

We were involved in reparations. Germany had to give up things like boats to pay for the war. We had to escort these boats from different ports to Denmark and East Germany. I remember once we had to pick up some Army personnel; we didn't know what for. We were anchored off a small island while these soldiers went ashore. We hadn't got a clue what they were going to do. We were sunbathing on deck and all of a sudden we noticed a puff of smoke on the hill. In no time at all we were showered in debris and a gun barrel came sizzling into the sea not far away. Of course, we all dived down the opening in the deck for cover. They were blowing up an anti-aircraft installation; never told us, we'd no protection or anything.

I was demobbed at the end of 1946. It was more difficult coming back to Coventry than going into the Navy. All your thinking was done for you in there. If you had to go somewhere you were given a warrant, no expense involved. I did miss the comradeship. A ship becomes very much a part of you. I couldn't settle down for a long time. Everything's flat when you come back. The war was over and the reception you had at one time was all finished with. No-one really wanted to know. My parents didn't seem all that concerned, I wasn't a Douglas Bader or anything. We had an important job that had to be done and we were there to do it.

The spirit onboard ship is entirely different, you never really shake it off. I did for a long time, but it came back as strong as ever. I couldn't define that feeling. Once a sailor always a sailor.

# PART FOUR

# WOMEN AT WAR

# A Few Feet Closer and We'd Have Gone Up

## The Story of Grace Golland

Grace Golland was born in Longford, Coventry, in 1920. She worked in the family fish and chip shop in Much Park Street before being called up at the age of twenty-two. Grace served on gunsights on what was called radio location: following German aircraft and relaying information to the guns. During her time in the ATS she received the British Empire Medal from King George VI for "courageous behaviour in danger, and consistent and unsparing devotion to duty".

If this is it, this is it, I thought when I got called up. I went all over the place, always on gunsights miles from anywhere. We just took it, you've got to do it and do what you're told. The attitude of the men towards the women was all right. They'd make facetious remarks at times or do a bit of cussing and swearing and you'd swear back at them. Most of the gunners were really pretty good.

We sat in a cabin. They were only small, it was very narrow to walk in because it was full of instruments.

There were four of us girls in there. I suppose it was a bit claustrophobic, but we never thought about it then; we'd be doing it all day and every day. I couldn't do it now, I'd come out screaming in five minutes.

I had headphones on and sat facing the instruments. The woman next to me had to get what you call the bearing of the plane — where it was coming from — the next one had to get the range — how far away it was, or how close — and the woman on the end had to get the angle. The instruments were supposed to mix all this up and come up with a position for the aircraft. I'd be on the telephone to the officer in charge at the command post and he either gave orders to the guns to fire or didn't.

The girl sitting next to me used to wind a handle and as she wound our whole cabin used to go round. There were aerials on top, God knows how far up, 30ft or so. We had to do our own maintenance and I was mad enough to go up there and clean those aerials. You had to be careful but somebody had to do it. We used to have climb up there like a lumberjack.

When I was in Kent we used to have a hut and when we were on manning (on duty), we could go to the cookhouse and get supper but if the phone rang then you knew — out you had to go as quickly as possible. The sirens had probably gone in Sittingbourne.

We wore trousers on site, but if you got a pass you had to wear a skirt. Ooh, those awful stockings, heavy, thick lisle things. They looked horrible. Why we thought they looked better inside out I don't know. There was a thick seam right up the back and we probably thought that the seam made them look good. If you got caught when your stockings were on inside out you had to go back and change them.

One thing that used to amuse me was the way they did toast, I've never forgotten it. They had cookers that ran the whole length of the cookhouse. I can see it now, this big black range. Someone used to come along with this stiff yard brush that they'd cleaned the floor with and sweep the top of the cooker with it. Then someone else would follow up behind her chucking slices of bread on to its top and that was toast! I reckoned I didn't like marmalade when I went into the Army, but I soon learned how to. I didn't like baked beans either, but I learned how to like them as well. "There's two things you can't spoil," I thought.

*Towards the end of the war Grace was posted to Belgium.*

Heck of a place that was. Belgium was dreadful. Snow everywhere. I couldn't write any letters because in those days there were no biros, you had a bottle of ink and it was just frozen solid by the side of my bed. We used to pile into a lorry and go to the nearest town for a bath. There was a tiny little village with about four houses in it and what they called a bistro. It had a dirty great notice in the window that said "English spoken". All he could say was one word, "Goodnight", that was the English! That was Joe, everybody called him Joe.

I've never been so cold in my life as I was in Belgium. We slept in Nissen huts. I can remember now lying in bed having been on duty and icicles were hanging down from the roof. We had stoves in the huts, but if we wanted wood for them we had to go and cut our own from the forest. Some of the officers were sneaky. They'd come round and if they thought you had too much wood they used to nick it for the officers' mess. We used to come back and go to bed and shove a couple of logs in the bed with us. It was the only way to hide them.

The incident I got a medal for happened in Iwade, a little village between Sittingbourne and Sheerness. It was towards the evening and was really an attack on the gunsights themselves, we were most definitely their target. It was the only real raid that we ever had on the sight. They never came back.

Inside our post we hadn't got a clue what was going on and couldn't hear what was happening very well. If I'd heard explosions I'd have probably run a mile! The cabin we were in was on a concrete stand surrounded by a wire mesh mat. The following morning half the gunners on the gunsight were on their hands and knees digging out incendiary bombs that hadn't gone off, and of course this mat thing had got holes all over it. When we came out we could see rubble everywhere and the damage to this mat. We were very lucky, a few feet closer and we'd have gone up. Aren't I lucky! We'd have gone in and done the same thing the next night, though, without thinking about it.

These medals, they're not exactly a misnomer, but I think the three other girls with me deserved it as much as I did. It was just I was what they call no. 1 and they were 2, 3 and 4. We all just carried on, we didn't think about it.

I can't remember much of what the old king said to me when I got my medal because he had an awful stammer. He was really very nice, but I just couldn't tell you what he said. He had a long queue of people and you just sort of walked up, stopped and stood in front of him. All I said was "Yes, sir." I felt very nervous. I had to curtsey and those ATS skirts weren't exactly what you'd call voluminous. I was frightened to death I'd end up on my nose. I didn't, I made it, but it was all over in a couple of minutes. My whole family came with me to Buckingham Palace. I think my mum must have been proud, but she didn't make a fuss, my mother wasn't like that. It was just "Oh well, that's another job done, get back to life now".

I think a lot of civilians were in more danger and had to put up with more than some of us in the forces. We didn't have to bother about ration cards; even if you couldn't eat the food, at least there was some. There were people going into town after the blitz and they'd see a couple of queues and say "You join that one, I'll join this one"; they wouldn't know what they were queuing for. I should think there was more hardship among the civilians in some ways. I think if anybody deserved medals it was some of them.

# 5,000 RAF and 80 WAAFs

## *The Story of Irene Edgar*

Irene Edgar was born in Earlsdon, one of ten children. At fourteen she left school and worked at the Standard Motor Company where she trained as a comptometer operator. Against the wishes of her father, on her eighteenth birthday she enlisted in the Women's Auxiliary Air Force.

I was not very happy at home. My father was very Victorian. We weren't allowed make-up, boyfriends, anything like that. He was not averse to giving you a beating, and of course when I got older, towards the age of eighteen, I resented this. My mother used to say to me, "If only you would keep your mouth shut, you wouldn't get into so much trouble." I tried at seventeen and a half to volunteer for the services but at that age you needed your parents' permission, so of course there was no way! My mother would have let me go but my father wouldn't. At the age of eighteen you could go without your parents' consent, so on my eighteenth birthday in 1944 I went down to Warwick Row and volunteered for the WAAFs.

I told my mother after it was done, because I knew there was nothing they could do about it then. I realised my call-up papers would arrive eventually and that I would have to tell my father before then. We had no privacy. If letters came to the house he would open them even if they were addressed to us. Mother used to shield us as much as she could, but she said "You have to tell your father because the letter will come." So I did. He threw me out — then, that night. He went for me and I'd had enough, and I must admit I went for the poker and I said "If you come near me I'll hit you with this." He said "There isn't room for me and you in this house. Out." I was going against his wishes, you see, because his word was law.

*After being thrown out by her father, Irene stayed at the parents of a friend for a month until her call-up papers came.*

My call-up papers came and I went off to Wilmslow in Cheshire. There were other Coventry girls going. Funnily enough, I didn't think I would be homesick, but for the first few nights I cried myself to sleep. I realised I did miss my home. I wrote to my mother and one of my sisters, so contact was made. In actual fact, we made it up, and when I had leave I went to stay with the family. It was an uneasy truce. My father never asked me what I'd been doing, but we got on all right.

I was at a big RAF camp with a contingent of WAAFs and RAF recruits. You did what they called square-bashing, in other words you were put into shape. We were in Nissen huts that held about twenty-eight and you were issued with a uniform. There was a coal fire each end for your heating. It wasn't really warm, but at that age you've got young blood flowing through your veins and it's all very exciting. There was discipline, lights out at a certain time, kit inspection, polishing your bed space, cleaning all your cupboards and everything. We were lucky in the WAAFs, we had sheets, the men just had blankets.

*After training Irene was posted to the RAF records office at Barnwood in Gloucester.*

I worked in an office. My job was replacement, transfer of troops; if they had a vacancy for a sergeant I'd have to allocate one from somewhere. I won't say the RAF men at Barnwood ever made me feel really welcome. There was a certain amount of prejudice towards the women's forces, but we felt we were doing a good job. The Glorious Gloucesters, who had just returned from Burma, were very nice when they moved in. They used to invite the WAAFs to their dos. After they left the Americans came. We didn't know why, nobody knew that D-Day was about to happen. These were the first Americans I'd seen. They were great! Their uniforms were smarter, they'd got chewing gum, nylon stockings. Two of the girls got engaged to them. When we were invited to their dances the food was something out of your dreams. We had a lovely time.

One of the manufacturers from Coventry provided sanitary towels for the women's services and it used to be on the notice board in the guard room "STs in". I remember one particular night, just before D-Day, I had a date with an American and he was walking me back to the guard room and he said "STs? What are those?" I couldn't for the life of me say sanitary towels. "Saccharine tablets," I said! I got back to the hut and told the girls, "Saccharine tablets for our tea!" An inspiration.

During the war I learned that underneath the surface there is no difference between what they call the upper classes and the lower classes. In my hut in Gloucester there were bunk beds. By that time they'd started conscripting women and the lady below me, Frederica, was a conscript and was considerably older than me. She mothered me, because at the age of eighteen I really was very green. She said to me one day, "Monty, (my maiden name was Montgomery), how would you like to come home with me one weekend?"

"Ooh Freddy," I said, "That would be lovely." So off we went to London. We were met by a chauffeured car, taken to St John's Wood, door opened by a butler, a maid to take my greatcoat. It turned out her father was chairman of some fantastic firm and they were fabulously wealthy. They couldn't have treated me better. They made me completely at home, they embraced me.

It didn't matter what you had, people were people and there really were all sorts. There was a real spirit of camaraderie. In the winter we'd all sit round these two coal fires in the hut and exchange stories. One night we were talking about what we did before the WAAFs and this girl said "Oh, I was a prostitute, but I thought I could do better in the forces". We really did laugh, she was so nice.

*When the war ended Irene, now a corporal, served in Germany working in the denazification programme.*

There was a vacancy for a corporal comptometer operator in Germany. I said to my sergeant, "Any chance?" She said, "If you want to go, post yourself." So I posted myself out there.

It was a horrendous journey to Germany. The trains were like cattle trucks and we were all standing shoulder to shoulder, airmen, soldiers, WAAFs, everything. We travelled through various German towns that had been bombed to pieces. I must admit, and I'm not always proud of these thoughts but I was still only twenty, I felt vindicated for what had happened to us. Having come through the Coventry blitzes when our family had nowhere to go (we had no Anderson shelter and just sat under the table or wherever we could throughout the whole lot), I'm afraid I didn't feel any remorse at all. I just thought, "Jolly good, we got our own back." Our cathedral at Coventry meant a lot to me and it had been horrendous to think of all that destroyed, so seeing the German towns bombed like that didn't particularly perturb me. I just thought "Jolly good, now you know how we felt."

I visited Berlin while I was posted in Germany and it was bombed to pieces, terrible. I saw Hitler's bunker and we went round his Chancellery. Well, it had been fairly badly damaged, but as you went in you could see the mosaic on the floor, white with a huge black swastika in the centre and as the guide was talking I picked up a few bits of the mosaic which I've still got as a memento.

The longer I stayed in Germany the more sympathetic I became towards the ordinary man in the street. Their spirit was very low. I did find it in my heart to realise that in their own way they'd gone through as much as we had. My job was in the denazification office. Germans who were known Nazis were brought in and interviewed. I made notes, taking down what was said. It was sort of dog eat dog; perhaps somebody would report someone else as a Nazi as a way of getting back at them. It was up to the officers that I worked for to sort the wheat from the chaff, assessing people on the information available.

*Irene met her husband while serving in Germany.*

We'd travelled over to Germany in battledress which is not the most flattering attire. We were all very tired when we arrived and the officers sent us for a cup of tea in the NAAFI before we unpacked. I walked in with a couple of other WAAFs and there were 5,000 RAF and RAF regiment men on that unit and about 80 WAAFs. There were quite a few weddings actually. I saw this man and he couldn't take his eyes off me. I said to my friend, "He'll know me next time he sees me," and never thought any more of it. A few weeks later one of the girls in the office said, "I've got someone who wants to meet you." I went along and I was introduced to this man, who I married eleven weeks and six days later. His friend who acted as best man said that he had said to him as he saw me walk into the NAAFI, "That's the girl I'm going to marry." We were married for forty-two years.

*Irene's husband wrote the following poem to her when they were both stationed in Germany and still boyfriend and girlfriend. She has it framed on her wall at home in Coventry.*

> *To A Lady*
> I write this to a lady
> to whom my heart is given.
> For one sweet word of gentle love
> I'd waltz my way to heaven.
> I wish that I could sing her
> The song that haunts my heart,
> The muffled painless thumping
>     that she alone did start.
> But one fine day I'll tell her
> just what she means to me,
> and if she tallies with my heart
> 'tis in my arms she'll be.
> So blessed be The Air Force,
> through them I first did see
> the sweetest girl called Irene
> who means so much to me.

We made a vow that on our golden wedding anniversary we'd visit Israel and walk the Via Dolorosa. Unfortunately, my husband didn't make it. A couple of years after his death I said to my son, "I have to do this for your dad," and I went to Jerusalem on my own. The Wailing Wall has got little cracks in it and you pop a prayer in and the rabbis take them out and attend to them. I put a little prayer in and I spoke to my husband and said to him, "I'm doing this because you're not here with me physically but walk with me, luvvie," and I started walking. Well, we always used to hold hands, I never put my arm through his; we always held hands and he held my hand and we walked the Via Dolorosa together. It was the most wonderful experience, actually feeling that he was walking there with me. I felt very uplifted. His name was Walter.

# Our Pauline Wouldn't Do Anything Like That

## The Story of Pauline Leslie

Having grown up around Earlsdon and Cheylesmore, Coventry's blitz forced Pauline Leslie out to Rugby, and it was from there that she joined the Auxiliary Territorial Service, aged twenty-three. She became part of the first all female regiment, the 93rd Searchlight Regiment.

I was working at William Brannigans in Much Park Street where they made all the badges for uniforms. They wanted to keep me there, it was a reserved occupation, but I wanted to join up. I don't know why I wanted to volunteer, except I wanted to do something more than work in an office. My father had served in the Navy throughout the First World War and I had wanted to go in the WRENs, you had to have some connection with the Navy, you see. I went to Birmingham and had the medical for the WRENs, but when I got to the interview they only had vacancies for cooks and orderlies. Well, I didn't want either of those jobs so they said, well you'll get called up for the ATS then.

Seeing as I'd been a shorthand typist, I assumed I'd be a shorthand typist in the ATS. I ended up volunteering for a new regiment that was being formed, the 93rd Searchlight Regiment. A Royal Artillery officer gave us a talk about it and he said, "In years to come they'll say 'What did you do in the war, grandma?'" It was the only regiment in the world, at that time, completely comprised of women.

My parents weren't very thrilled about it. They thought I was just going to be a typist. Women didn't wear trousers much in those days and my mother walked into town from Orchard Crescent and she saw this big Army lorry and girls in trousers jumping out of it. She said, "Not my Pauline, my Pauline wouldn't do anything like that." Of course I did! She said she hardly spoke for a month after I joined up, she was so upset to know what I'd let myself in for. She was really worried. Funnily enough, the day I joined up my only sister joined the Land Army.

We had to go on what they called a toughening-up course first, in Rhyl. We were sent out into Wales and had to find our own way back with map references; there was drill of course, and aircraft recognition. After that we were posted to different sites.

The trains were always packed when I came home on leave. I'd have to sit in these compartments, the only girl surrounded by all this uniform. The train was stuck for ages once near Coventry station and I remember I just opened the door and climbed up the bank.

The regiment had so many batteries; I was in 342 Battery. There was a sergeant, a corporal, a lance-corporal, that was me, and ten privates. They were all women, the only men we saw were when they came to do maintenance on the searchlights. We all had a number, I was no. 6. I'd be under cover at the back with a screen in front of me. If the girl in the open saw aircraft she would notify us and shine the light on it. I'd be inside getting the messages through on the radio transmitter, no. 9 would keep the generator going — we had to have a generator because we were out in the wilds, you see. Then we had a dispatch rider who went from sight to sight.

*In 1943 Pauline was stationed in the Home Counties.*

In 1943/44 there weren't any enemy aircraft in Hertfordshire, but we had a message on the RT saying some planes were coming over but without pilots. They were V1s and V2s, Doodlebugs. We were sent down to Kent to shine the light on these V1s and V2s when they came in so they could be shot down. I couldn't tell my boyfriend where I was going because it was all very secret.

I remember one occasion on my off duty night. I was completely on my own because it was only one person off per night. You were more scared then than when you were on duty. Well, I heard an engine overhead. If it went quiet with those Doodlebugs you were in trouble. I heard it stop and I got under the bed. That was a direct hit on Orpington. I was quite scared that night.

The Americans were stationed near Hemel Hempstead manning the Flying Fortresses, the American bombers.

When you saw them parading they were nowhere near as smart as our British soldiers were. They arranged for us to go and see where they were stationed and we climbed all over these Flying Fortresses and saw these planes that they were using for bombing. The lance-corporal on that sight married one of these American soldiers. I remember being on duty with her and all night long she played this record, a love song for her American husband. I often wonder if that marriage lasted.

I met my husband, Sandy, at a local dance, he was stationed near Hemel Hempstead in the REME. We got married in November 1945 and went on honeymoon to Devon. We'd arrived on the Sunday and by Tuesday night we had a telegram recalling him to India. Wednesday morning we'd booked an early breakfast and were on our way back to Coventry, just in time for him to put his uniform on and get to the station. I never saw him for a year but he wrote to me every day.

When Sandy came back we were all set to go and live in his home town, Aberdeen, but there was more work here and so in the end we decided to stay in Coventry. There were no houses available in the city and we were in rooms in Humphrey Burton's Road with a baby by now. It didn't work out at all and was a very unhappy time, because of all the people to own the house it was a German couple, and they'd be chattering away in German in the kitchen while I was trying to get the baby's food ready. It was an awful start really. We applied for a licence for one of the new houses they were building. There were 200 issued in Coventry and we got one. Once we knew we were going to have a real home we came away from those rooms and stayed at my parents. Every weekend we used to go and watch the bricks being laid on our nice house. I never regretted joining up. I had a marvellous time and I met my future husband.

# PART FIVE

# NORMANDY

On 6 June 1944 the *Coventry Evening Telegraph* posted up news in its office windows. The Allies had landed. The City Council held a minute's silence and prayers were said at the cathedral as Coventry men, along with thousands of others, began their assault on the beaches of Normandy.

# They Called Them Stormtroopers

## The Story of John Barker-Davies

*John Barker-Davies, a captain by twenty-one, served in 46 Royal Marine Commando. A D-Day veteran, he fought with his men in the Battle of Rots against Hitler's fanatical 12th SS Panzer Division Hitlerjugend, in an effort to push the stormtroopers out of Caen in Normandy. His war ended in India as he waited to go into Burma.*

I rather fancied the Royal Marines. You had a great choice there: you could go to sea, do ordinary soldiering, even go underwater. They called me up for my service in January 1941. I was twenty-two when I went over on D-Day. We went over in two cross-channel steamers. I was quite excited, not nervous; it might have been helped by the fact that there was a bar on the ship!

I was in charge of sixty men. We landed on the junction between Sword Beach and Juno. We were late because the Germans had these large gun batteries, some of them with 500 Germans in. We had to wait and see if they were going to open fire and knock the ships out of the water. Whether you liked it or not the chap that jumped out first was an officer. Certain boats had foundered and they couldn't get ashore. You could see men drowned in the water, one or two who had tried to swim and been pulled down by their heavy loads. It was a bit rough.

Most of the casualties on the beach had been cleared. Your aim was to get away from that area, put your head down, go as fast as you can and take cover at the top, then get enough men together to knock out any resistance. We had to get to the coast road. There was a large gun firing down at us; we encircled this and all packed in, took about fifty prisoners, no trouble at all. A lot of them weren't German, they'd been pushed into it and they weren't very good soldiers. I think they were relieved to be captured.

The first few days in Normandy were very hectic. Every day you'd got something to watch out for. I think you're better in your first attack. When you've done one or two, you don't like it so much because you know what to expect. It was very nasty in the early days. The Germans had some very good guns: the Schmeisser, which is a type of German tommy-gun, for example. It could cut a chap almost in two. In actual fact, I got one myself and used it because I found it much better than our tommy-gun and it fired so many bullets. In daylight you were always under shell fire and mortar fire. You hoped for the best and took what precautions you could, spread people about so you didn't get too many casualties. But men get experienced at this, it's what they learn. They save themselves.

88

I never thought about death at the beginning, but you get to think that it's loaded against you in the end. When you've done one difficult job there's always another one to go out on; there's a hill to be cleared and then there's another hill and you're not so sure any more. You've got to be prepared to run all the risks and you'll find in that sort of unit the officers take an awful belting. We were very, very short of officers in no time at all.

It was miserable in your trench. You had to put wood and bits on top of your head to stop it getting wet. You'd got to keep your eyes open at night. We didn't expect to get gassed, but you had a gas cape as well. Mind you, after the war I could sleep anywhere. I used to sleep in the waiting room at the railway station. When I came back to my Law Society examinations I walked it. I could stay awake until two in the morning and be perfectly all right, I'd got used to that sort of thing.

After D-Day + 1, we were pushed out down towards Caen with the Canadians and I was ordered to go to a radar station that was occupied by several hundred Germans. I led a Bren group, that's three men with a gun and my batman, down to a track towards the radar station. I left the rest of the troop in all round protection near the roadway. It was a bit difficult because we knew we were being observed, but we went on just to see what we could find. After about 500yds we saw a barricade across the roadway. It was manned by two Germans with a machinegun. They were just waiting to let fly at us and that's what they did.

A chap called Corporal Cherry got badly hit. I pulled his body behind me and to the side. He was moaning. We were too exposed to move, but I shouted to the Bren group who were on the other side of the road, "Get up and run as far as you can. Get down into some corn." They got as far as the corn and they were all right. After about an hour there were boots on the road. The Germans came along and fired shots at me lying in the grass. They took my batman prisoner. They thought I was dead.

Our padre walked down the roadway; they didn't fire at him. He picked up Cherry and got him away. He got the DSC medal for that. Cherry survived and used to phone me every New Year's Day until he died. My batman was a prisoner for ten days. He was freed when we captured the radar station, but he never fought again, his nerves had gone.

I knew they were going to shell this place from the sea and they shelled it while I was lying there, 15in shells, but I wasn't hit. I had to move. It didn't get dark until late on. I edged away a bit at a time and got as far as the corn, got myself in the middle of a great big hedgerow and slept like an animal. The Bren gunners had made it out and I slept there till it got fairly light and crept out from there.

I thought my men were excellent. The difficulty with being an officer was that you couldn't be as pally as they could be with each other. If you'd got a decent sergeant major you could get on there. I wasn't too austere, but you had to be sensible, do what you think is best for everybody and look after them.

There were moments when it was more difficult to forget what I had seen. I had to write letters to wives, you know, bad news. You couldn't get a lot of time for those things; you'd got so much to think about, your ammunition, how you were standing to stop the enemy coming through. At the start of Normandy I couldn't write letters at all, it was so hectic. When we were relieved and taken back I could write at my leisure. You'd be as sensitive as you could, try and do a decent job. I still feel very close to my men. One of them is still here in Coventry, a very nice chap. They're all dying off now.

You had two types of patrol: the fighting patrol which was about thirty men and the recce patrol which was just two or three men going very carefully and getting information. We had a lot of patrolling to do at night. You'd meet the Germans half-way and sometimes they'd fire and sometimes they wouldn't. Same for us. What was rather nasty was all the dead cattle lying feet up all over the place. When you walked along a hedgerow you'd come across one of these things in front of you and you couldn't see what it was. Bit nasty.

One of the difficulties was that when you came back through your own lines, some of our people got a bit nervy and seemed to forget we were out there. You were very lucky not to be knocked over. I came back myself from a night patrol; I'd warned people I would be coming back through their position but the captain in charge hadn't told them, so one of their blokes was about to shoot me. Then he said, "I've just recognised you!" Even in the dark — lucky he knew me. Really lucky.

*John remembers 11 June 1944 when 46 Royal Marine Commando fought the SS, pushing forward to liberate the villages of Le Hamel and Rots. The battle was a particularly bloody one, and John's men soon discovered the fierceness of the Hitler Youth Division. All day 46 Royal Marine Commando fought against the Panzers and the SS Panzer grenadiers. After a street-by-street battle they liberated both villages. The following description is from an eyewitness who visited Rots the day after the battle: "The dead lay corpse by corpse. Here is the confirmation of how ferocious last night's battle must have been. The Commandos lie dead in rows beside the dead SS. Grenades are scattered all over the road and in the porches of houses. Here we see a Commando and an SS man, literally dead in each others' arms, having slaughtered each other."*

There were a lot of little battles which I could forget about, but quite frankly the Battle of Rots with the 12th SS Panzer Division was one of the nastiest. We were under the command of the 1st Canadian Infantry Division and our aim was to drive the Germans away from Caen. The Panzer Division was comprised of the Hitler Youth. They were very good, vicious. They called them the Waffen SS Stormtroopers. There was a heck of a difference between the ordinary German soldier and the SS. They were fanatics. They'd come at you even though they'd lost a lot of battle casualties.

There weren't many Englishmen about, most of the men were Canadians, who were excellent — first class.

We were about 440 strong. We only had about four or five tanks, American ones. They were good and quick, all right for going across country, but the German Tiger tanks were huge things and the Panzers could knock things out like nine pins; all our tanks were knocked over.

My sixty men and I were making our way up this orchard. I went forward with four or five blokes down as far as we could until the Germans attacked. We ended up at that point with several casualties. Two of our chaps were still alive lying in the road and we fired beyond them. We couldn't do anything for the chaps who were dead. We got those wounded ones, picked them up and doubled back. Very nasty, you expect something in your back when you're running, but you've got to get the wounded out of the way. The troop on my right was going through a cornfield, they went for it and they got done for. A lot of blokes including the officers and four of their sergeants in that troop were killed. One of the chaps, a first-class bloke just on my right-hand side about 40yds away, he got a phosphorous grenade. Awful thing. He was shouting, screaming "Shoot me". I didn't like that, I must admit. It was very nasty. That troop had nobody left to look after them, so I was put in charge of those men as well. We had to hold our position there and not retreat.

We waited at night for them to attack and we were all ready for them. We didn't really have time to get dug in properly; we prepared a place as far as we could. We were absolutely exhausted. We tried taking rest but we couldn't. Forty prisoners from B Troop had been taken that day. [They spent the rest of the war as prisoners.]

One of the SS officers stopped the others from machine-gunning these captured men. Anyway they took the green berets from those marines and threw them back at us that night time to taunt us. It had been a nasty day. We'd killed 122 Germans.

I will say that the next day I had to go and bury our people and the Germans didn't fire a shot. Ten men went with me and the padre (who ended up marrying me and my wife). We couldn't be sure that they wouldn't shoot but we took a chance. Those dead men were in that resting place until they were taken out and buried in the Bayeux cemetery. The French Canadians buried the German dead, all 122 of them.

We buried our men in the orchard, just going into the village. It's nasty burying men like that, very sad. I mean people's livers dropped out and God knows what. If you'd been hit with one of those German Schmeisser submachine-guns it could tear a man through like a piece of jelly. You just had to go on with it and do your best. I still think about those memories from time to time. After the war I'd be asleep on a train and dream about that battle. My legs would jerk up. It gradually went away.

In the hamlet of Le Hamel, the area where the battle took place, there's a monument: "In proud and everlasting memory of the men who served in 46 Royal Marine Commando who laid down their lives in Normandy, Holland and Germany."

When you're in battle it isn't like cowboys and Indians, but it isn't far off. There's a tremendous roar of noise and God knows what and then it goes dead quiet. You mustn't walk down the middle of the road, you have to go from one house to the other, hiding. Before you move you've got to look for a sound base where they can't hit you and before you get up you find another one, somewhere you can dive into and not get shot. When you kill someone yourself it's just "bang" — you don't think about it.

I was blown up by a mine on 30 June. I had a horse to ride for a while in Normandy and it got wounded by mortar bombs. We had to get rid of it, it was a pity. I went out to get a new horse, a great big German one it was. Some chaps seemed to realise they were in danger and had a feeling they were going to be killed. I had two or three cases like that. There was this one marine, he was very nervous that day.

"I don't know what's wrong with me," he said, "I feel nervous."

I said, "you come with me to get this horse and I'll look after you."

I was pulling the horse by its halter, and unknown to me the field we were walking through was mined. This nervous chap was throwing mud at the horse, walking about 30yds behind me. The horse went over a mine and it killed the marine. I was by the horse, but he was the one it killed — the blast went up in the air and then down — "bang". The horse was split in two and I was covered in horse blood. I got it all along here, my shirt was gone, there were bits of shrapnel. I felt fairly calm though. I was able to walk back to my unit and even chatted to them. The shock came on later. They took me to the airborne dressing station. I was put down as very seriously wounded. They thought I had a real chance of snuffing it. I had penicillin every three hours from when I was examined until I got to the Bradford Infirmary two or three days later. I didn't go back in until the end of September. The other chap is buried in the airborne cemetery.

*On 11 June 1987, forty-three years after the Battle of Rots, Captain Barker-Davies had a reunion in Normandy with the German veterans.*

I met them in Bayeux and rightly or wrongly I invited them to come to our cemetery. There was a lot of stuff in the press saying we shouldn't be meeting up with them, but my padre who had been there at the battle said, "Blow the rest of them. We'll do it." I took what was left of 46 RM Commando to their cemetery. I was very embarrassed actually, because we didn't think they'd come but they did. They'd brought a great big wreath and I'd only got this small arrangement! I rushed all round the cemetery looking for the German graves and fortunately I found about 500 of them. It wasn't all total forgiveness, but we were polite, never taught to be anything different. They gave me a huge book too, which I shall be leaving to the Royal Marines. It's inscribed to 46 Royal Marine Commando from the 4th Company 12th SS Panzer Regiment.

I met Hubert Meyer there. He was very big in the SS. After the leader of their division was killed in the battle he was second in command, the Chief of Staff of the 12th SS Panzer. My wife met him in Normandy and she said he gave her the shivers. I was going to buy them a beer in Bayeux but they all wanted a cognac! And their wives. I had to pay for it!

We couldn't get the Germans to leave, I think they wanted to stay all night. Anyway, I was lucky to take Bill Millin to this reunion. He was Lord Lovat's piper and had played on the beach on D-Day. So we got Millin to play the Germans on to the bus with his bagpipes. It was the only way to get rid of them!

*Captain Barker-Davies has received several letters from Hubert Meyer and other members of the 12th SS Panzer Division since the Reunion. Here is one of them:*

Dear John,

When I am in my pub and talk to the guests and when there are German soldiers in uniform, I often think of the meeting in France. They were wonderful days and evenings. But in the year 1944 there were bad days and nights for you as my enemy, and for me. But we do hope that our governments will be so intelligent that no war will come again for our countries.

Best wishes to you and your comrades,<br>Hans Diekermann

# Am I in Heaven?

## The Story of Jack Hawkes

Jack Hawkes was born above the family shop in Earlsdon in 1917. Called up in 1940, he served with the Royal Warwicks and was posted around Britain on defence work, spending 1942 and 1943 training for the push back into Europe. While Jack was stationed in Yorkshire he went into the 185 Infantry Brigade, which was preparing for the invasion. It left for Normandy on D-Day + 1. Jack's war started, however, at Budbrooke Barracks in Warwick.

The funny thing was everybody said "Whatever you do, don't go to Budbrooke". Well, I had a letter to report there on 15 January. We got a travel permit from Coventry station to Milverton in Warwick and thirty of us marched through there to Budbrooke. You saw these barracks looming in the distance. It was a dreadful place, like a prison. We went into this room which would normally house thirty men, but it had sixty in it. You'd have a bed and then there were three wooden planks and a couple of wooden trestles in between, so there was virtually no room. You had to take a canvas bag to the barn, fill it with straw and that was your pillow. You had two coarse blankets. You can imagine me, the only boy with three sisters. I was ruined! Being hurled into this lot, oh it was dreadful! The food was a bit of a shock to the system. Breakfast was sausage, which was pretty well raw, and for tea this chap would come along with a bucket of hard boiled eggs and just spin them down the table!

The thing that really shook me most about Budbrooke was that there were four men in the platoon out of thirty who couldn't read or write. Chaps had to write letters to their wives for them. They used to put rather naughty stuff in sometimes, terrible things! No matter what, everybody had good points. The roughest of the rough were the diamonds in a lot of cases. You might not believe this: some of them said "This is the best life I've had", when they got into the Army and had regular food and clothing, "Oh, the best life I've had for years".

*Jack was part of the Normandy landings. He went over for the invasion on D-Day + 1, 7 June 1944.*

You had this horrible feeling of "what the Dickens is it going to be like?". Just dumped on a beach that was heavily defended and that was that. You become fatalistic really: what is to be is to be. To be honest, I don't think anybody thought they'd survive, that's how you felt. We went from George V Docks in London. We were loaded on to an old Swedish coal barge. They'd planked all the hold over and the carriers were lifted in. We went over sitting on the deck. You really were terrified about what you were going to come up against, but it was fascinating to see all these warships and boats. The channel was absolutely choc-a-bloc, like Piccadilly Circus, and there were the planes of course.

We were winched off our boat to go ashore on Sword Beach. The beach was secure, the fighting had moved inland. All these heavy cruisers were firing 17in shells on what they thought was the German position. The track vehicle that communicated with the Navy had been blown to smithereens, so it really was chaos. They were firing off nautical rocket launchers, about twenty or thirty at a time, and of course there was aerial activity as well. Yes, it was noisy.

Unless you've actually been in it, you can't imagine the smell of a battlefield. The Germans had a terrific amount of horse transport, they didn't need petrol you see! Well, all these horses were slaughtered, lying there killed — apart from the men of course. Dreadful, dreadful. That's what stays in your memory the rest of your life.

I was in a carrier platoon. Two sections went on D-Day and two on D-Day + 1. If I'd gone on D-Day I wouldn't be here, because the other sections were either taken prisoner or killed. We were the only support weapons the battalion had left. When I landed, Sergeant Jackson, who had been sent back to the beach, said to me, "It's terrible up there. The battalion's pretty well wiped out. It's almost like another Dunkirk." They'd been sent up this ridge when it wasn't secure. The Germans were battle-trained, we were raw; they must have thought it was madness going up that ridge.

All these poor chaps had gone up the lane, a natural tank trap with a wood at the top and a crossroads, a Tiger tank down each side of the crossroad. The Germans let all of them come through and then it was over. When we took the ridge a month later our carriers were up there, and some of the poor devils were still in them. The Germans hadn't bothered to bury anybody. Our colonel was killed on that attack and he was still lying under a hedge a month later.

That's what I got when I went ashore. We had to get as much ammunition as we could off the beach. They were just dumping it any old how, it was very haphazard and we had to go and sort it out. "Get what you can because we shall need it," Jackson said. They put what was left of us on a little ridge and the order was "You just stop here". It was like the old Wild West days, last round, last man.

*Jack spent one month here taking part in night and day patrols in an effort to secure Lebisey Woods.*

They were mortaring us and shelling us all the time. Conditions were a bit grim. You were in view on this ridge and you could hardly move without being seen. You had to use a bit of fieldcraft. Sometimes you were patrolling, trying to find out what the Germans were up to. You didn't want to be captured by those Panzers; they did obey the laws of the Geneva Convention to some extent, but not always. They could shoot you.

I remember the first day-time patrol I went on. We came back and went along this hedgerow which gave us

**101**

cover right up to the wood. Once you were in the wood you could get back into the battalion position out of sight. Our officer said, "Come on, we'll make a dash for it." Of course, the Germans had mortars and machine-guns set up on fixed lines and as soon as we got into the wood it was "pap, pap, pap". I thought, "Here it comes," and we dived into this gully. There was a Coventry chap lying by the side of me; I'd got my arm up here and he'd got his leg down there and I felt his leg jerk about 6in from my head. When it was all over and we got up to go he said, "I can't get up, Sarge." I said, "What's the matter?" He said, "It's my leg," and there was this tiny hole in his trouser leg. We ripped the trousers, and from his knee right up to his crotch was all open. We were only about 300 or 400yds away from the battalion position, so they brought out a stretcher bearer and took him back.

You slept in your trench. That's your home! In three months I only slept with a roof over my head twice. You'd dig a slit trench round the edge of a field, you'd have a Bren gun or something in position there. You can't do too much to your trench because you don't want to be spotted. You'd be in there at night and then every morning at dawn you had "stand to" when you got in position in case an attack came. If ever a major attack came in, it was always at dawn.

You lived on field rations; you had a wooden box called a fourteen-man pack — enough for fourteen men for one day or one man for fourteen days. There'd be a tin of bully beef, tinned sausages, tinned bacon, toilet paper — very thoughtful! I always remember the

Ambrosia rice. The chaps who landed on D-Day had these tins of soup with a sort of Roman candle down the middle. The candle burns down, you open the tin and you've got hot soup.

You washed when you could, out of a mess tin most of the time. If you were in a village that hadn't been too badly damaged, there'd be piped water. When we moved into areas where the Americans had been, we used to go on a scavenging hunt, because they had these great big packs of food. They always had more than we did as regards rations and they used to throw half the stuff away.

Normandy is a wonderful dairy area and they had all these lovely cattle. The brigade commander told the farmers to get most of them in, but they wouldn't. Our chaps had to put down anti-tank mines in a hurry, just laid them all out and these blessed things were wandering around blowing themselves up. The whole area was littered with dead animals. That didn't smell very pleasant either. The cattle would blow up like balloons with their feet in the air and eventually they'd burst.

*Jack lost a lot of his friends during his time in Normandy.*

Just imagine half of your friends disappearing almost overnight. They send up reinforcements but it's not the same. I remember one Earlsdon chap, Lewis, he was nice, I knew him well. He was killed putting out anti-personnel mines, these blessed terrible things. The

Germans saw our men, mortared them, and instead of lying still they panicked and ran, and Lewis set off one of the mines he'd just laid himself. He was twenty-four.

If you were in a forward position and chaps were killed they'd wrap them in a blanket and put them in the rear area where the supplies were brought to. When rations were sent up they'd take the bodies back. They would allocate fields for burial. You had two discs with your Army number on round your neck. If you were killed one of these stayed on the body and the other went back to records so they could advise your next of kin. I remember one dreadful place over in a château where our burial parties were burying Germans. The Germans started shelling us and a chap from my platoon had to dive on top of this German to get out of the shelling. He had to lie on top of that body for about an hour while it was going on.

You can't imagine the debilitating effect shelling and mortaring has on you day after day. They're terror weapons, meant to demoralise you. You'd think "Where are they going to start today?" Mortars were the worst. Every day you had it. Set times. You'd say "There's a stonk coming in". You got philosophical. "If there's one with my name on it, that's it." You'd get chaps with arms and legs blown off. You hope you're not going to be mutilated, if you're going to get it, that it's going to be clean.

*In September 1944 Jack was wounded in Holland.*

We were on the western flank of the Arnhem Bridge head area preventing attacks coming in from that direction. There were these little slit trenches on the roads covering the outskirts of the village and in the morning the company commander came round and said "Go forward and tell them we'll try and get some rations to them within the next hour". I started walking up this road just after dawn.

The Germans had these six-barrelled mortars and you'd learn that they went one, two, three, four, five, six — so if the first one landed over the top of you you'd be all right, but if it landed in front you were in trouble because it was like leap frog. Well, I heard this thing start up and it was obviously targeted at the road I was on. I dived into this alleyway, thank God I did, and I lay absolutely flat. I heard it, one, two, then a hit in the road opposite where I was; it left a great big hole. I was covered in dust and I got up and thought "Phew, am I in heaven or am I still here?" I walked up to the forward position and stood right on the edge of the trench. This chap said, "What's the matter with your leg, Sarge? You've got a great big hole in your trousers." When I pulled my trousers up there were two clean holes, one either side of my leg. I hadn't felt a thing. "A decent night's sleep! A week off in the rear!" I thought.

I finished up being sent further and further back on these trucks the whole day and ended up in the main hospital in Brussels. It was full of casualties, Americans and our chaps. There were Germans too. There wasn't any animosity. You just looked at each other. You were all in it. They were just ordinary chaps like us who probably didn't want to be there any more than we did.

I went for surgery the next morning. They had to open the leg up from two points. All the muscle had been shattered inside and it had to be cleaned out. The next day I was on a Dakota from Brussels to Swindon, flown back home. They unloaded us on to ambulances as all the early morning rush hour was going on in the station. I finished up in Derby hospital. Being taken out of everything so suddenly, I thought, "Am I really going to make it now?"

*After six years' service Jack was demobbed on 22 February 1946. He was issued with civilian clothes — a suit, a shirt, a pair of boots and a hat. On 1 April 1946 he collected his gratuity from Earlsdon Post Office: £80 for his six years.*

When I came out I missed the enormous brotherhood. Almost immediately you came home you had to pick up the threads, but you missed the company of these chaps. I'd been with them for six years. Of course, a lot of them were killed or wounded or we got split up, but you always mixed. There was spirit among everybody, you were all in the same boat. All that disappeared.

It all comes back to you on Remembrance Day. The Legion send us one of those crosses every year and we fill in the name of one of the chaps that were killed who we knew. They put the cross outside Westminster Abbey.

We gave up six years of our lives. I lost the wonderful opportunity of university. The war was our university. Mind you, it was a marvellous thing for life to teach you. It helped me to be tolerant, to deal with things. I've been down to the very bottom. I thought, "Whatever happens from now on, it could never get any worse than this".

# How Terrible War Is

## The Story of Arthur Mills

Arthur Mills enlisted at Warwick in February 1944 when he was eighteen years old. After training for the invasion he left Portsmouth on D-Day + 2 for the Normandy Landings. Serving in the infantry, Arthur fought in Europe until the end of the war.

We went from Blackpool where we'd been training down to Portsmouth. We didn't know what was going to happen, but we knew that we'd all got to do our jobs and our bit. There were about forty-five, forty-eight of us, all youngsters. Our gang that went were all the same age, all from Budbrooke Barracks and from around Warwick and Birmingham. The Americans supplied us with a very good meal and we all went off by lorry down to the waters for embarkation. All the women and children were waving and off we went on a destroyer to France. They needed more infantry you see, got to keep pushing on.

We landed at Arromanches. Quite a few of the boys were nervous, a bit edgy. When we first got there we saw these German prisoners being loaded on to the boats we'd just got off. I felt like kicking them into the sea. One or two of our lads shouted, "it's all right for you. I wish I was going home!" The very first action I saw was when somebody shouted "Get dug in! Get out of the way!" and one of our lads went *walking* across and was killed outright, no hanging about. He'd only got married three or four days before. I realised straight away when that happened that you'd got to look out for yourself.

I was amazed by the volume of our troops. There were divisions of Canadians, of Polish, and there was to be a massive assault on Caen. We were to be assisted by literally hundreds and thousands of fighter pilots and bombers and all these troops were going to move slowly up. The Polish were doing the guns and we were to start this very big attack to drive round to Caen.

We'd all got a little yellow triangle on our packs so that the planes could see where we were. You'd flick them over your head and just tie them on. Loads of planes came in from England to help us. We were all very pleased to see them, but we suddenly realised they were taking us as well, although I've never heard it said officially. We were all standing there waving our yellow flags and they were firing at us. Everybody was trying to scatter. I threw myself under an armoured vehicle to try to hide out of the way. There was a reconnaissance plane weaving in and out and he stopped them.

We came through the fields and dug ourselves in at the edges of roads. The planes got round to Caen, all these bombers pouring over and we just sat there watching all the bombs fall. It was such an awful, awful shame because Caen was a beautiful little place and we just watched it destroyed. I thought, "How terrible. How terrible war is".

We started off getting into a routine of making little attacks. The Germans would do something and we'd have to go round and get stuck in. It was no good panicking, I suppose you were always hoping it would soon be over. You learned things as you went along. For instance, the tanks joined us up by Caen. I thought, "Get behind a tank". I didn't realise the Germans fired at the sound, they weren't looking for us, they were after the tanks. I soon learnt: don't walk behind a tank!

Whenever Field Marshal Montgomery came, we'd know there was something going on. He'd got a very squeaky voice and he used to say, "All gather, gather round. I want you to do something for me," and we'd all think "aargh!" because we knew there was going to be some special attack going down.

We were always pushing on at the Germans. We had to kill them as we came across them. That's infantry, you see, you just kept on going. It's a hard do. You couldn't just go walking about nicely. You'd go round a corner, see a field, a hedge, trees or something and you didn't know who was behind it. Killing didn't bother me at all. Once you'd seen your own lads killed you'd got no softness for the other side. When you lost someone you'd hear "So-and-so's had it". You didn't have time to feel sad about it in the middle of an attack, but when it was over and we were assembled again it would hit you, although you couldn't help feeling "I'm glad it wasn't me". The most distressing thing I saw was in Holland. A group of fellas, who should have been dug in for the night, were missing. We finally caught up with them and they were all dead, tied to the trees and shot. Very distressing.

There was a team of blokes whose job it was to bury the dead. It was a department way back of us. There was the odd occasion when there was no-one there to help us, so we buried one or two real mates ourselves. German prisoners were sent back down the line too. As to how I felt about the Germans, well, I was just looking forward to knocking them over. We used to call them terrible things! It was all about supporting one another, you had to help each other and not let one another down. We made very close friendships; it was sort of necessary really. When there were no Germans about, we'd sing to cheer ourselves up and tell rude jokes.

When an attack was over we'd get dug in every night, make sure we were covered. You'd put your feet up, have a rest, but you'd have to be quick. When the Germans came you could hear them within minutes. You'd be digging in, a bit of shelter of your own, and you'd hear the German planes. They used to do it regular, used to shower us. There were a couple of blokes who got killed going to the toilet outside one night. We'd been told to go to the toilet inside the building we were sheltering in, but they'd gone outside just to make it more comfortable and got shot.

On my nineteenth birthday I ended up on this little island. Tanks had lowered these great big ramps down and we had to run over them to get on the island. The Germans soon realised that we were on there and they kept shouting at us that they didn't want to fight. Well we got dug in, but were eventually woken up by a bloody horse and cart coming round the corner; it was Germans but I don't think they were soldiers. We stopped them and took the horse and cart off them. In the light we could see a church. They were bringing the dead to bury — we realised we'd dug down in a cemetery. It was 5 November and there we were among all the dead.

There was one occasion, we were in an outhouse in Holland and the Germans were on the other side of this road. There was one German, I'm not joking, he was a giant. He used to get up every morning and have his shave. We liked it nice and calm with nothing going on and wanted to keep things quiet so we took no notice of him. Well, this sniper was brought in. He said to me, "I've been ordered to shoot him," and he did, from a church tower. He shot this German and that was it, all hell broke loose. The Germans started shelling the church and smashing everything inside to get this sniper. We ended up with everything coming at us. It was nice and peaceful before that, but things couldn't stay that way, it was war.

They wanted me to be a sniper because I was a very good shot. I'd been shooting in the countryside all my life with my dad, killing rabbits or whatever, and when I got to Budbrooke Barracks I found the shooting part easy. You could refuse to do that job though and I did refuse. It wasn't for not killing Germans, it was that you'd be putting yourself under stress. Snipers had to push out and go in front on their own sometimes. So I was the man with the radio, I always had it with me. It was my job to gather all the information from different sections and pass it on to the officers. I remember when we got caught by German mines. One had been set off, it hadn't actually killed anyone but had badly injured some of the lads. There was a lot of "Everybody, for God's sake, keep still". We knew the Germans weren't that far away and we could see some of them round the back of this big farmhouse. I had to radio our position as quickly as I could and call for assistance. I gave our coordinates to a gunner who was some way away and finally they cleared the Germans out. That was the sort of situation you didn't want because you couldn't do anything yourself.

The closest I came to an injury was a bullet that hit my helmet, deflected and knocked me to the ground. We were just about to start an attack when the Germans got in first with a mortar and an officer was injured. I had to pick him up and cart him back to the small building we'd started from. The sergeant major said, "Well done, Mills. Go and give 'em a hand, catch 'em up," that sort of thing. I thought I'd get to have a cigarette first! Well, off I went again, but by the time I got back there were none of our soldiers left. They were running across the field and up the slope towards the village. Then, of course, this German started firing at me and clipped me on my helmet, knocked me over. The others started shooting back at him and I finished my running!

I can remember liberating towns. The Dutch were very, very thankful to us when we'd got them all cleared. The families we came across always came out with a little bit of something for us, a bit to eat or a drop of milk. Mind you, there was one Dutch girl who was friendly with the Germans. Our section was receiving a lot of shells and a lot of damage. We couldn't work out how the Germans were managing to get such accurate strikes. We found out that this girl was passing back information at night about where we were dug in. That sort of thing happened once or twice. At times we came across German houses and the people were holding up white flags, surrendering. We didn't do anything to those.

I saw the airborne divisions at Arnhem. We were watching it all, watching them pouring over, coming towards us. We thought it was great to see them. But, of course, as they were coming down they were just being slaughtered and suddenly it was a terrible sight. On another occasion we had to cross the bridge at Nijmegen over the Rhine. It was a big place, we could see the British taking a hammering, but we couldn't get to them. By the time we could help them the Germans were scattering, but you ran like crazy over that bridge, you ran really quick. The Germans were having a go at us, I went like lightning!

*Arthur married Betty in 1949.*

I remember the nightmares Arthur had. He never talked about the war at all when we were first married, but we never had a night's sleep without him thrashing all over the bed. It took him years, years until he was able to sleep well. These days he would have had counselling, but there was no such thing then. I had no idea what he'd done during the war. I think he wanted to shut that part of his life off. I think he needs to go back to Normandy, it would lay a few ghosts.

*And a final few words from Arthur.*

I never talked about what I'd seen and done in the war, it just wasn't something we spread about. We just got on with life. I'd know that this mate and that one had lost his life, that so-and-so was gone. I'd think about it but I'd never talk about it, not even to my own boys when I had children. I've got it all inside me. I might get upset sometimes because I've got a terrific amount of memories — they come back at you. I found out one thing: there are a lot nicer things to do in your life than go to war.

# PART SIX

# IN THE DESERT

# The Horses Came First

## *The Story of Harold Hancox*

Harold Hancox was born in Cow Lane, Coventry, and grew up in Cheylesmore. He added a year on to his age and joined the Warwickshire Yeomanry as a territorial in 1937 when he was only fifteen and was called up aged eighteen. Harold rode his horse until animals were replaced with trucks, Jeeps and tanks. He served all over the Middle East and North Africa.

At the start we hadn't got any horses, so they commandeered them from bakers, milkmen, hunters. They just went to the stables, paid the owners so much money and took the horses. Some of the owners would start crying. "Look after him," they'd tell us.

In 1939 we were in Sherwood Forest doing schemes with the horses when the order came for us to load up on trucks with the animals and we were taken down to Dover and then across to Dunkirk. We put the horses onto French cattle trucks when we got over there, eight horses to a truck, four on each side and two men in the middle. It was terrible, because horses will fight, you know. They bit one another and kicked. You'd hold up buckets of water for them to drink from and it would all dribble down on you. We were freezing. I saw tin helmets flying out of trucks, kicked out on to the road by horses.

We went down to Marseilles where these boats had come in from India carrying Indian troops and mules. We had to clean the boat out before we could get on because they hadn't mucked out at all. It was a terrible stink. Then we were off to Palestine through the Mediterranean. The Med can get very rough; a lot of fellows were seasick on that journey including me. At one point a gale started up and sixteen horses were drowned with the waves coming over the side. We just had to chuck their bodies overboard.

We used to get potatoes in their jackets to eat; well, they didn't just have the jackets on, they had the roots on too! Of course, when we slept up top we wouldn't be in a hammock, we'd be lying on the deck. There would be water sweeping along the surface mixed with muck and urine, very uncomfortable, terrible. We used to throw the horse muck straight over the side into the sea, but then we were told that submarines could follow the trail so we had to load it up in bags that would sink to the bottom. I was a trumpeter, but they stopped me playing reveille on board because they said the sound would carry, and of course we couldn't be spotted.

*Harold eventually arrived in Palestine where, after eighteen months with horses, the Warwickshire Yeomanry became mechanised.*

It was hard work with the horses: you've got to groom them, water them, feed them, exercise them, muck out. The horses always came first. They were very expensive and men were ten a penny.

We were patrolling the wire between Syria and Palestine, and Saturdays and Sundays you had night guard-duty. They'd bring you down a bucket of hot cocoa and bread and cheese for supper and then you'd have to saddle up in the dark and go patrolling round. I knew all the bugle calls on my trumpet. You had a different call for every order: a horseback charge, mount, dismount, ride at ease, reveille. There were lots of them. I couldn't read music but I learnt it all by ear. I had to remember all of them.

The horses were terrified of camels; if they saw one they'd bolt. If a horse died in Palestine we just had to throw it over the cliff face. The scavengers, vultures and wild dogs, would clean them all off. Within a couple of days the horse's body would just be bones. But you can't fight a war with horses. Eventually when we got to Jerusalem we got rid of them and replaced them with trucks. I felt a bit sad getting rid of my horse Ben, but they were hard work. Some of the lads from the countryside outside Coventry felt it more when their horses went. They'd grown up with animals. To me it was an adventure to be mechanised and I found it quite exciting. I handed in my trumpet and became a dispatch rider.

One of my Coventry school friends was killed in Damascus by the Vichy French. It was June 1941. There was this huge fort which we couldn't take because we hadn't got the big artillery or any aircraft, so we bypassed it, but a Coventry troop was ordered to stay. The Vichy French came out in an armoured car with white flags. Our men saw the flags and thought it was safe. They got out of their trenches and walked towards the Vichy French who pulled the white flags down and opened fire. Seven lads were killed from Coventry including my schoolfriend. The rest were taken prisoner. When we got up towards Damascus I went up and saw my friend's grave and when we came home I visited his mother. When we were in Iraq we had to be very careful moving off in the mornings because the Vichy French used to bomb us. We used to form a square out of all our trucks and get out before it was light and the bombing started.

Driving thousands of miles through the desert in a truck was hard, but you were fit. The Germans had bread but we didn't, it was all hard tack. These hard tack biscuits were thick and square and we used to put them in a tin and boil it and then add a bit of jam, stir it up and call it biscuit duff. We had meat and vegetables in tins. We used petrol to boil up our tea, because out there in the desert it was cheaper than water. You'd get four gallons of petrol in a square tin and we'd use these empty tins. You'd cut it down, put a handle on it and when we wanted to boil up we'd put some sand in the bottom of the tin, put a bit of petrol in it and light it up. When I was a dispatch rider and I needed petrol they'd chuck me a 4-gallon drum up. I'd fill my bike and what was left I'd throw away; it was that cheap, you see.

You had to make your own entertainment in the desert. We used to play rugger and football. We played the New Zealanders. As for going to the toilet, you'd just go off and dig a hole somewhere. We had this brigadier and he took his shovel out into the desert one night to go to the loo. You'll never believe it, but he came back in with nine German prisoners at the end of his shovel. He pretended it was a weapon and they couldn't tell in the dark.

I went down with malaria about four times. You start to feel all cold and shivery with it. When we were in Persia four Coventry lads died with it. Just before Alamein I had two attacks. I was put on a hospital ship and was treated just outside Haifa. I managed to get back to the regiment about two days before Alamein started.

During the attack it was my job to follow the tanks in; I was in a Jeep. We'd move up at night. The barrage would start up: there were flashes, shells, tracer bullets, firing all over the place. This went on for three days and all night long. Of course you were frightened.

The dust and the sand were terrible. The Sherman tanks had an aeroplane engine inside them. When they revved up they'd dig a right hole in the sand. If you were following one of them you couldn't see a thing. If one of them got blown up they would explode right out into the air because of the high octane petrol they used.

I had a mate with me and we were taking messages from one place to another. We got to a place where the tanks were all down and we were running between them. The tanks had been knocked out, but not

**123**

everybody was killed because they'd baled out. They'd dug holes in the sand for protection. We drove round and picked up any men we could and brought them back. Our Jeeps were empty and we could fit a few blokes in, I managed nine once. They were in a terrible state, shook up, covered in dust and muck, some of them were injured.

We lost a lot of tanks, so they pulled us out until reinforcements arrived. We attacked again and that was the famous Operation Supercharge. We went in with 160 tanks and came out with about 10 or 11. I was still in the Jeep going around picking men up. It started to rain and the desert was like a sea, it was amazing. The tanks were all right and my Jeep was ok, but the soft-skinned vehicles with the ammunition and food couldn't do anything and the three tonners with the ammunition got stuck. I never had to fire a shot in anger. I was frightened but it was the lads in the tanks that had it rough. I've got the greatest respect for them.

*Harold was demobbed in 1946, after six and a half years' service.*

I had the Freedom of Warwick when I came home. That's where I go on Remembrance Day, that's where our roll of honour is. To me the war was an adventure. There were some bad things about it, but there are places I've been that I would never have seen. I was in hospital in Nazareth, I was in barracks in Jerusalem, parts of the world I would never have imagined going to.

**124**

# Tanks Through the Minefield

## The Story of Les Ryder

*Les Ryder had already been serving as a territorial in the Warwickshire Yeomanry when he went off to war at the age of twenty-two. He was a dispatch rider in the Middle East and North Africa, most memorably at El Alamein.*

My father was in the First World War and within twenty years of it ending I joined the Warwickshire Yeomanry as a territorial. It had to be the Yeomanry with the flash uniform, the jingly spurs, riding horses every weekend; we used to gallop around with swords drawn.

There were five of us working at Morris and on 1 September 1939 the foreman came round and said, "switch off your machines and report to barracks." War was declared on 3 September. It was my wedding anniversary, not a happy day. I was outside Quinton Road Barracks with a sword in my fist and the sergeant major came out. He said, "It's your wedding anniversary, go home. Be back at twelve." It was 6 o'clock, so my wife and I had six hours together. Sunday morning we were on parade and we listened to

**125**

Chamberlain tell us we were at war. Three days later I was off to Nottinghamshire and I didn't see my wife again for five years.

Out of the five of us who'd worked at Morris, one died in Persia, another was captured by the Persians, one was wounded at Alamein and me and another lad were OK. The one who was captured was led with a rope round his neck following a mule with everybody laughing at him. He never got over that.

It was a bit of a blow to come from home and your nice bed to sleeping in stables: cold floor, a pillow full of straw and a couple of blankets. The regular Army would be in barracks, but we just had to make do. We got horses from all over the country, tied them to these horse lines. It rained, it was cold, it was miserable. I went in the canteen in the evening and I told this corporal, who was a friend of mine, what I thought of the place. I'd been riding a bike since I was twelve and this corporal knew it, because I'd raced against him and we got on like a house on fire. The next day I was transferred to the signals troop as a dispatch rider and I ended up as a troop sergeant in charge of the scout cars, Jeeps and bikes. They were the biggest load of bolshies you'd ever met in your life, but that was the sort of bloke you wanted for the job.

There were no flash bikes in the Army; we used civilian ones painted khaki. You didn't have all the bull as a dispatch rider, none of the parades and all; you pretty well had a free hand. We didn't go around with big guns shooting at everything, but wherever the tanks or any action were, you'd see a dispatch rider. The radios weren't all that ideal, a lot of them were from the First World War. The signals operatives were brilliant to keep things going.

We had an excellent signals officer. He let us get away with murder. We taught him how to ride a bike. He was very good, quite over-exuberant. We told him that even good riders wouldn't attempt the things he did. I used to ride all over Palestine on the bike. I got to know it better than I knew Warwickshire. When the little Arab kids heard a bike coming they'd get as many small stones as they could and roll them across the road just to see what you did if you fell off.

We had to go a long way back to get water in the desert. You couldn't go forward because you were in enemy territory and you didn't know where the wells were, so you went back. You had 200 gallons for a regiment to drink, wash, look after the vehicles, fill the radiators, so you're on about a pint a day. They say you can't live on that, but at the end we got to the state where we didn't sweat. We just adapted to it. Those kids were as tough as old boots. After six months our skin looked like leather anyway, we were as brown as anything. We were all terribly fit, even though we basically only had tinned bully beef and biscuits. After a bit Australian food came up, and you'd get tinned potatoes and stew, which everybody liked. But the cooks never came up anywhere near us, they were miles further back. You just ate when you could. If you were in a truck you'd eat on the go. We'd have a packet of biscuits and a 7lb tin of marmalade or jam and you'd dig in as you were driving. At night time you weren't allowed to light a fire, so it was cold tack. The last people to come in were the water cart people, the dispatch riders who were riding around trying to find out who had broken down and the poor old fitters. Their truck would be miles behind repairing broken-down vehicles and they wouldn't get in until midnight. All that and nobody grumbled. They all had jobs to do and they were covering their mates.

When we went into action at Alamein I was in a Jeep. You'd go in a team of two vehicles so that if one got knocked out there was still the other to get on with the job. We'd got about 800 guns a mile away blasting everything, aircraft going over, shells everywhere. There were flares dropping all around and ack-ack guns knocking them out of the sky. The whole atmosphere was like this. We used to drive between the infantry and the tanks, climbing all over the place. Just in front of us there were two 3-ton open trucks full of shock troops who could jump out and support any infantry gaps where they were losing. We were with the 2nd New Zealand Division then and it wasn't very often you'd find holes with them. We couldn't believe it when a Jeep pulled up behind one of these infantry trucks and told them to put their fags out. Right in the middle of everything. We howled at that.

Eventually we had to stop. We couldn't get through any further. There was a German 88 gun somewhere on our right and the crack of it was a different sound to any other gun. The four of us just leant up against our Jeeps drinking scotch out of tin mugs while all this was going on because we couldn't do anything. We were as

**128**

scared as anything. Although we'd been in three campaigns before, Iraq, Syria and Persia, this was the first real action we'd seen.

We were stuck in the middle of a minefield at one point with tanks on either side getting blown up all around us. Some of the bravest men were the ones walking across those fields. In front of us would be some poor bloke with a compass, all on his own walking across the desert towards the enemy. He'd have a white tape tied to his body, a bloke 8ft to his right and another 8ft to his left. They would walk to make a channel through the minefield. That takes as much bravery as it does to fly a Hurricane. If this man got killed another would take his place straightaway. They'd got to keep going, you see. They'd got to make it through the minefield. Quarter of a mile behind him, blokes would be prodding the ground with bayonets looking for mines. They had tin hats painted white on their belts and they'd drop them wherever they felt a mine so the guys behind them could lift them away. It took time, as they had to feel all around and be very careful, because there could be a wire leading from one mine to another. These lads had so much bottle. We watched one go past and he never stopped, he just kept going.

On the second day we were there we'd dug our slit trenches as quickly as we could. We didn't know if the regiment was in front of us or behind us. Tanks all started coming through the minefield and flaring out and going up this ridge, and as they made their way up it was "bang, bang, bang" on the mines. You're as scared as the next bloke. My friend Hank actually saved my life. Just as a Sherman tank went down into our slit trench he pulled my ankle and dragged me out of there. I would have been crushed. Nobody thought anything about it at the time among all the commotion that was going on. Hank told me it was an automatic reaction but we're very close to this day. I knew all the blokes in the Warwickshire Yeomanry personally. Even now, after sixty years, we feel like a family.

# PART SEVEN

# THE WAR WITH JAPAN

In March 2001 I wrote to Ron Hadley, Branch Chairman of Birmingham's Burma Star Association. His reply explained a good deal about the conditions for those men who served in the war against Japan. Parts of his letter are reproduced below.

Dear Caroline,

Your interesting enquiry and request for information is acknowledged and it is hoped that this reply will be of assistance to you in your quest. The Burma men consisted of each of the Services: the Army and the Royal Navy, the Royal Air Force and also Combined Operations. Behind the enemy lines were units known as Chindits [the Burmese for Lion] who engaged in long-range deep-penetration warfare and you may possibly meet some of those men who served with Wingate [Major-General Orde Wingate, 1903–44].

Many men who were posted to serve in the Burma campaign were of the Royal Warwicks although they were transferred to other serving Regiments upon reaching the Far East. They all served as infantry of the line, under arduous and inhospitable conditions, where serious privations and risk of jungle illness became the norm. This, you will find, is most likely one of the reasons why men are not eager to discuss with strangers of the past years. Such men, mostly of your grandfather's age, will occasionally talk amongst themselves about their exploits because "they were there" and there is a keen rapport and understanding of life as it was accepted when they had no choice but "just got on with it". As someone unknown to them you will need to exercise patience and, perhaps, some perseverance to gain their confidence and engage in meaningful conversation.

# Something More Than the Norm

## The Story of Ron Johnson

At a Burma Star service in Coventry I was lucky enough to meet Ida Johnson, widow of Burma veteran and Chindit, Ron Johnson. Although Ron was no longer here to talk to me Ida told me small pieces of his story. The feeling I had was of a man who had held in a lot of traumatic memories and suffered in silence over the years. Below are some fragments of his three years in Burma.

Ron was born in Godiva Street, Coventry, in 1920. At the age of twenty-two he was called up into the Army. His brother Stan had been taken prisoner at Dunkirk in 1940 and was to remain a captive of the Germans until the end of the war. The boys' mother said she spent her time waiting behind letterboxes desperate for any news of her two sons. Ron would never talk about his memories, but Ida managed to gather small bits of information over their forty-year marriage. His own nephew didn't even know his uncle had served in Burma until five years before Ron died. Documentary makers approached him, but he could never agree to participate, always saying it was too painful an ordeal to recall his past.

His training in England was so rigorous and demanding that he had some suspicion he was up for something more than the norm. In 1942 he was posted to Burma where he remained until the end of the war with Japan. He served with the Leicesters in the elite Wingate's Chindits, a unit equivalent to the SAS of today. Fighting deep in the Burmese jungle, Ron battled with a stubborn and cruel enemy under hellish conditions, sometimes remaining in the jungle for stints of up to six months. The men in Ron's section were flown in on Dakotas, their mules flying with them, de-tongued so as to make as little noise as possible and kicking madly at the walls of the aeroplane.

Ron slept where he could on the ground, battling with snakes, insects and poor food. The men would burn leeches from their bodies, find them in their boots and even had to fend off bands of stick-wielding baboons on one occasion. Years after leaving Burma he still suffered vivid nightmares where he would jump out of bed and brush imaginary snakes from his body; he would see them everywhere.

One of the most distressing memories Ron had was of him and five others in the jungle. One of the men was lost and the other five went back to look for him. Eventually they found him hanging from a tree, ankles tied together and wrists bound, shot through the head. Ron said he was a lovely lad, just a young boy.

Sometimes the stench from dead mules and dead bodies was so terrible that the men had to tear off pieces of parachute material to wrap over their noses in an effort to block out the smell. He remembers one instance when Japanese soldiers were moving up towards the British on the edge of a river. The British fired and killed the enemy. The next day they found the Japanese soldiers still in the same positions in which they had died, some propped up against their swords, "like a museum," Ron said.

Only a third of the Leicesters came back out of the jungle. Ron went on to suffer bouts of malaria all his life, having had a very severe attack of the disease while serving in Burma. While recuperating in hospital from that attack, Ron was in such pain he felt himself rise up from his body as if he were going to die. His hearing also remained bad, Ida thinks, because of the amount of the anti-malaria drug quinine he had taken. Ron couldn't work for twelve months after he returned to England. He was too unwell mentally and needed to recuperate. His brother also returned from his POW camp and their mother must have had her work cut out looking after her two sons.

Ron never softened towards the Japanese. When a young Japanese woman attended a Burma Star meeting one month, he refused to go: up until the day he died he could not forgive their actions during the war. The Burma Star and Chindit Associations played an important role in Ron's life. Here were men who knew what he had been through and seen. Whenever Ida hears the Last Post she tells me she is filled with pride and emotion. In Ball Hill at the church which the Coventry branch of the Burma Star attends, Ron's name is carved into the roll of honour along with those of other dead veterans of the war with Japan. Every man in his branch attended his funeral. Ida tells me her husband was a handsome man: "He had the loveliest hair. With his gorgeous sweep of grey hair he even looked beautiful in his coffin."

# He Died on the Spot and That's All There Was to It

## The Story of Alan Roberts

Alan Roberts was born in Hillfields, Coventry and volunteered for the Army aged seventeen. Having completed his training at Budbrooke Barracks in Warwick, he joined the Royal Engineers and was eventually posted to the Command Operation school in Troon, Scotland, where he served as an instructor in explosives. After training for the pre-airborne division and completing officer cadet training he was posted to the Far East where he took part in special operations against the Japanese.

I went to Chesterfield, did all the practising, dropping off walls, rolling over and dropping off backs of lorries. It was all right, but no worse than the assault courses you always had to do. But then they sent a group of us to Manchester, to Ringway Airport, for airborne training. The first drop was the scariest because you dropped out of a balloon, you actually had to leap out of the basket. I've got a head for heights, but at 800ft you can see every dog, it's too near the damn ground. It was automatic so your parachute opened immediately, but you were really scared. You needed a new pair of underpants! We had to do ten jumps in total. We went up in Dakotas and jumped from them at about 2,000 to 3,000ft. You sweat a bit, but there's a sergeant by the door and he throws you out; if you hesitated you got this shove in the back. I'd done my eight day time drops, but before I'd had a chance to do the two night drops I was sent to Newark for nine months' officer cadet training.

*After finishing his training at Newark Alan, now a second lieutenant, was posted to the Far East.*

When I first went to Burma it was exciting. The first thing you see when you approach Bombay is the sky changing from a blue to a sort of curry yellow over India, because it's all dry and the dust rises up; and then the smell of the spices comes out from the shore about 50 miles away. We arrived through the gateway of India all pink cheeked and in our khaki uniforms.

If you were going into the jungle for special operations you had to have three skills. Mine were explosives, languages and paramedics. I'd been sent to Madras medical college for six months to learn the paramedic stuff and field surgery. Field surgery in the jungle is cruder, it's a bit like the Napoleonic wars for amputations. If somebody's wounded there's no hospital anywhere near so you've got to do something

**140**

about it. If they're slightly wounded then you treat them, mostly stitching and cleaning up wounds. They taught us to use maggots for cleaning up jungle sores, dog saliva as an antiseptic, as long as it didn't have rabies! The leeches could cause general sores, which then became ulcers and ulcers could kill. If a man was a lot worse, if gangrene set in, you had to do amputations and you needed anaesthetic. We used to have tins of what looked like toothpaste tubes filled with morphine. If you unscrewed the cap on the tube there was a needle and that became a hypodermic. There were six in a tin. One would ease pain, if it was severe you could use two. If you were going to do an amputation then you'd have to use three or four; if you had to leave a very badly wounded man, either the Japs would get him, and they weren't gentle at all, or the animals would get him, so if he was going to die and you had to leave him, then we gave him six.

The Japanese didn't wear heavy Army boots, they wore rubber ones with a slit between the big toe and they laced up so that the leeches couldn't get in. Our jungle boots were the same as we wore in Europe, big steel studs and eyelets, great for letting leeches through. When you marched the leeches would get squashed and your boots would fill with your own blood. Leeches leave their teeth in your flesh, so you should never pull one off because the teeth stay in and then they of course go septic.

Lice were a problem in the jungle too. There are several sorts and the worst one was the scrub typhus louse, which could kill you, so we all wore long trousers, not shorts. In the wet areas, the swamps, you got boring insects, things like jiggers, and they caused worms. You always got worms in the jungle. When you went to the toilet you would literally see something thrashing about, they could be really long. You were horrified.

We used to shave, it was part of our morale. We had cutthroat razors. That used to kill our lice. Our medical officers told us to wear trousers but not shirts. You sweated too much and you got the prickly heat. Your upper body would only be bothered by mosquitoes or ticks falling out of trees. If you had a tick you had to use a cigarette or heat your bayonet up, give the tick a stab and then pull it out of you.

You were damp all the time in the jungle. It was like being dipped in a mud bath. You'd get foot rot, fungus infections in the folds of your skin, yeast infections in your crotch. After the war, a Japanese POW showed me how to treat these fungus infections with tar off the road mixed with pig lard, it made a sort of cream. If I sweat I still get the fungus coming up even now, but I use cortisone cream these days!

My first mission was in August 1944. There were six of us on that one, a major in charge. None of us in the group knew each other except me and my best friend Geordie, who'd been with me through all the officer training and on the same troop ship as me. He'd gone off to another unit but we came together again for this operation. He was a sapper the same as me and they needed two sappers for the mission.

There was a very big prisoner of war camp north of Kanchanaburi (not far from the bridge on the River Kwai) where prisoners were sent from the Thai/Siam railway. They had wire surrounding the camp and they'd made the prisoners dig a big, deep ditch all the way round. On the corners of these ditches there were machine-gun towers. It looked as if they were going to kill all the prisoners. So groups like us were sent in. My job, together with Geordie, was to dig tunnels and then put explosives under the machine-gun towers at each corner of the ditches so that we could blow them up.

It didn't work out, though. It was just after dawn, we all had our submachine-guns, Sten guns and other weapons. I had a kit bag full of explosives attached to my leg: when you're about 30ft from the ground you let the bag go on a rope and it flops, and then suddenly you go slower. Geordie was carrying the detonators, because it would be fatal if I carried the explosives and the detonators: there'd be a tremendous bang!

The major dropped first, he was no. 1, Geordie was no. 2. We were all supposed to land on the east side and go up these mountains. But the major dropped too early, the wind caught him and blew him westward to the wrong side of the river, the west side. So he disappeared into the mist. I was last to jump because I had these explosives and nobody wanted me near them. Suddenly Japanese fire came up from the east bank of the river. I don't think they knew we were coming, I think the patrol was there accidentally, but they saw these parachutes coming down so they fired on us. They used tracers and you could see it arcing, it looks

**143**

like a hose pipe coming up. Anyway, they hit Geordie. He was carrying the detonators and he exploded. He was twenty, the same as me.

Nos 3, 4 and 5 were over the east side of the river by this time. I was the highest because I was the last one to jump, so I could see what was happening. I tipped my parachute silk shrouds to change direction. Before I came down, I threw away my submachine-gun to avoid drowning under its weight, same with the explosives; I just kept my jungle knife. I landed in the river towards the west side.

The other three who'd landed on the east were captured. They couldn't give any information because they didn't have any. They were executed. So it left two of us on the west side, the major and myself. The mist was on the river, I didn't know where he'd gone and fortunately neither did the Japanese. I swam to the bank, which was very muddy. I knew the Japs would come looking for me so I dug myself a little tunnel into the bank.

I hid in there for five days. It was like a rat hole. I had my emergency rations but that was all, and they were only supposed to last a couple of days. I was like an animal. I lived like a rat, I was stinking. You're not a civilised human being by that time. When I thought about Geordie, the only thing that kept coming to my mind was relief that it was him not me and that feeling was something I had to deal with later. I was determined to make it out. The need to live is what keeps your spirit up. You get used to it. You get used to it and you survive.

I was frightened, naturally. You mustn't be caught. I knew what they would do if they caught me. I stayed in for the first three nights. My training had taught me so well, I was always watchful; a slight noise which was unusual could alert me and I'd wake up immediately. Luckily there were lots of rushes and undergrowth, it was dense, but I could hear the Japanese on the bank.

I ate anything I could find, anything that moved. There are palm trees, rushes, roots. The Chinese eat lotus roots down by the water. You can eat leeches, snakes of course, but I could only eat things I could get nearby, terrapins for instance. The only thing was I couldn't cook, I just had to eat them raw. It wasn't too bad, we'd had to do things like that in training. Eventually I realised that nobody was looking for us any more, they'd gone. So I came out on the fourth night and started exploring, then went back in again.

After the five days I started making my way westwards; I found the track which ran parallel to the river. On the second day I was ambushed, luckily by some Burmese with the major. He'd been looking for me because he'd seen me coming down, but he thought maybe I'd drowned. The Burmese led us to a teak plantation about 25 miles away. It took us about four days, the jungle was very thick and we had to take care to avoid Japanese patrols. On top of that we were very weak by then too.

There was an Australian and an American at the plantation. They'd been teak planters and could speak Burmese: one was SOE (Special Operations Executive) and the other OSS (Office of Strategic Services). They had radio communication and they got us out. We were in a bit of a rough state by that time. I looked pretty dreadful, I'd lost a lot of weight and I was covered in sores. Absolutely exhausted. We spent about ten days there recovering and then the American and Australian escorted us to the coast. We were hidden in a fisherman's hut for a couple of days. We had to sleep on top of the fishing nets, it was absolutely stinking! At night we'd go out for a swim in the sea and try to get rid of the smell. Eventually a British flying boat came for us.

The only man I ever killed directly in person was a Korean. This was in April 1945 on the border of Malaya and Thailand. I was with a British Army Aid group on detachment with the Malayan People's Anti-Japanese Army. We were going through the jungle at night to blow up some Japanese stores. I was in front. We were following a wild pig track, but the jungle was very thick with a lot of undergrowth, thick bamboo and creepers and you couldn't see more than about 3ft in front of you.

This Korean fellow must have been on guard along the pig track but standing on the edge of it, because I couldn't see him there. I felt, rather than heard, something behind me and so I turned. The Korean lunged at me. He stuck his bayonet in my arm, I've still got the scar. Luckily it hit the bone and I twisted away with the bayonet still in so he couldn't pull it out and use it again (normally if you withdrew you could bayonet in again). I had my killing knife. I clapped my hand over his mouth so he couldn't alert anyone, which

**146**

was what we'd been trained to do. He died on the spot and that's all there was to it. We'd done the whole thing in practice so many times that you didn't think about it, it was an automatic reaction. He must have been a young man, about my age. I didn't know that until he was dead. I didn't have any reaction at all, you're just pleased because you're alive.

My feelings towards the Japanese? To us they were just a lot of soldiers. You don't hate them, you just kill them, that's what you're there for. I only killed one man face to face, as I said, but I blew a lot of other people up. The thing is, as with the bomber pilots, you didn't associate the people on the ground with the bombs you were dropping, or in my case, with what I was blowing up. In special operations you needed three things: supplies such as ammunition, medicine, somewhere to run and hide (the jungle in my case); and the hearts and minds of the people. Blow up what you like but don't kill anyone except the enemy.

My boss after the war had been a POW and he absolutely hated the Japanese as all POWs did. Actually, it was the Koreans we hated, because they weren't front-line soldiers and they carried out a lot of the atrocities on civilians. You could respect front-line soldiers because they were in the same position as you. I blew up about twenty-eight Koreans in lorries on the Burma road, brought the mountain down on them. The attitude was "a job well done".

*After the Japanese surrender in August 1945 Alan, now a captain seconded to the Indian Army, was put in charge of Japanese prisoners in Kluang, Malaya.*

I had my own company of 393 men and was in charge of 4,000 Japs in three camps. How the hell do you guard 4,000 men? They were the 110 Railway Construction Regiment and they were waiting for war crimes' trials. It was a question of sifting them out and seeing who they were. The British Intelligence and Military Police would carry out interviews. Intelligence is just talking to people and finding information, fitting it like a jigsaw. I only found about five vicious, nasty ones in the 4,000.

It was the easiest job I ever had because I was the boss and the whole principle of the Japanese Army was that you obeyed the rank above. Mind you, you had to tell them *exactly* what to do, they had no initiative. They'd been trained to follow orders precisely and if you gave an order it was carried out immediately. They were very afraid of their officers, so they were afraid of us. I was going round in the evening once and I found one Jap carrying bits of wood, shavings, etc. to make a fire for cooking. He shouldn't have been out like that. When he saw me he was terrified, grovelling on the ground, expecting to be beaten. I just sent him back, I wasn't going to hurt him or anything.

Their spirits were good, considering. Remember, they had been ordered by the Emperor of Japan to surrender. It would be terrible to disobey the Emperor, so they had the honour of obeying him — that was the

**148**

logic. We gave them back their "face" as well by referring to them as "Japanese Surrendered Personnel" and not "prisoners of war". They were in a good state physically because they had the same rations as us. We had a cigarette tin of uncooked rice a day (I was with the Indian Army now) and that gave us about two or three meals a day. The Japanese had the same as us. I even killed a few snakes and gave them to prisoners for food.

After the war there was an occasion when, as a student, I was working with one other man, about two o'clock in the morning, carrying stuff into this deep freeze, just the two of us. He was a German. We sat by the boiler to get warm and had our sandwiches together and we got talking. His career was identical to mine except that instead of fighting the Japanese he was fighting the Russians. He was at Stalingrad and he was in the Airborne. Two years before we would have tried to kill each other, now we were comrades. We exchanged experiences and talked about how stupid war was.

I've been a member of the Burma Star Association for a few years now. We mostly do funerals: each others! It's about respect for me. I go to the Cenotaph in the Memorial Park every Armistice Day. The principle is to remember people like Geordie. Normally you only remember the funny instances, but on that day you focus on the bad things.

Your success in war isn't due to organisation, it's due to luck. If you go down one path one day you might be OK. The next day you might go down the same path

**149**

and you've had it. It's the one that makes the least mistakes that survives.

I was completely ashamed and full of guilt that I felt no remorse for Geordie, only happiness that I was alive and it was him. This worried me for years and years afterwards: how could I react like that? But I've talked to other people and it's exactly the same for them — survival. Nowadays counsellors talk to everybody. With us, there was no such thing. I think counselling is wrong, it's confessions. You shouldn't take the guilt away, it should stay there within yourself. It does with me.

# When Will We Be Out of Here?

## The Story of Frank Rushton

Frank Rushton volunteered for the RAF just after his eighteenth birthday in 1942. Having served in England he was posted overseas in September 1944 and travelled all over the Far East, making his way up and down India three times. After a difficult eleven months in Sumatra, he came home to England five days before Christmas in 1946.

I'm the fourth son in a family of twelve. I'd already got two brothers in the RAF and at the time most of the men were joining up. I was fed up to the teeth of wandering round from one job to another and decided on my eighteenth birthday that I'd go down and volunteer.

In 1944 they decided it was about time we went overseas. We had an idea we weren't going to Europe. They sent us to Blackpool which was a kitting out place for the Far East and then gave us all the gear that was relevant like a pith helmet, which we threw away when we got to India. We had bush hats instead. The pith helmets were brilliant but they were no good for us in

**151**

the job we were going on; they were old fashioned, useless.

The boat going was a typical troop ship, thousands of blokes on board. It took twenty-one days to get there. We slept on deck because it was so warm. We only had one sub warning the whole time and that was in the Mediterranean. You just do as you're told and go where you're ordered. I was a gunner so I was on a gun post. Going through the Mediterranean was so beautiful. Not a cloud in the sky and the moon was absolutely brilliant, right down to Suez.

We were on the move a lot. I went up and down India three times. It was a hell of a place to travel, blooming old carriages and sleeping hard. When you got to your destination, unless you had some training to do, all you did was wander round, have a look at the place and then you were off to somewhere else.

*Along with the other men in No. 3 Flight, Frank was separated from the rest of his Squadron to take part in special training for a landing planned at Ramree Island on the coast of Burma. Frank kept a small secret diary and his short entries record his daily life in the days leading up to the landings at Ramree Island and events in the two and a half months he spent there.*

Tuesday 2nd Jan. 1945
Tents, camouflage and webbing dyed ready for operation impending.

*Wednesday 3rd Jan. 1945*
Dyed our clothing jungle green. Extra kit issued.

*Friday 12th Jan. 1945*
Have to pack diary and photos away, not allowed on this job. Nuisance.

*Friday 26th Jan. 1945*
Sighted our objective. Told it was Ramree Island. Invaded 5 days ago. Told to expect wet landing but wasn't too bad. Slept on beach. Heard guns shelling Japs.

We started sea landing training and minefield clearing. You had to be able to know how to clear an area with a bayonet and how to use dynamite and do explosive work. Once the training was over we got an idea that we were going to be part of the landings on these islands. The Army went in first and we took part in the secondary waves. We landed in the pitch black and spent the night in the sand dunes. We didn't sleep, we made tea on the tommy cookers. They were safe to use because you couldn't see the flame on them and we had these great little tea tablets that you just dropped into the boiling water.

Our job was to make sure the airfield was protected. We manned the guns and kept a look out for any Jap planes. I remember one pilot who flew over dropping shrapnel bombs, the type designed to cause maximum damage to human beings. We had a go at him, but he got away.

We slept out in the open all the time until we got tents. On the second night at Ramree I'd put my bed down on the ground near the guns and the next morning when I woke up I was covered in blisters all over my hands. I thought I'd got some terrible disease and went to see the doctor. You know what it was? Ants. Red ants had crawled on my hands and discharged this acid. You couldn't do anything about it, you had nowhere else to sleep. Those ants were the biggest plague you could get.

*Saturday 27th Jan. 1945*
Up early. Opened our 48 hour rations and brewed char with our tommy cookers, very dirty. Plenty of work, slept in the fields, on duty all night. Shelling but had tents up.

*Sunday 28th Jan. 1945*
Went to bed this morning, very tired. Japs trying to push on other side of island. Seemed like pretty big try, landed two of their Generals. Invaded Cheruba today by Marines. Duty tonight.

*Monday 29th Jan. 1945*
Feeling cheesed off. No mail yet, rations pretty deadly and no bread. Water situation pretty good. Landed other side of island, seemed pretty grim, lost a few men. On days tomorrow. Thank God.

*Tuesday 30th Jan. 1945*
Still no mail and am very hot on duty with Ken.

Orders to dig in. Naval shelling on N.E side of Island most of night.

*Wednesday 31st Jan. 1945*
Built shelter from sun. Still no mail. Wrote to Olive, first for over week. On duty all day. Spitfire pranged, no one hurt.

*Thursday 1st Feb. 1945*
Another Spitfire pranged. Pilot hurt but not dead. Rations improved but still no bread. On duty all night. Dug another shelter during night.

*Friday 2nd Feb. 1945*
Made a charpoy out of coffin stand from graveyard. Pretty comfy too. Wrote mum and Olive. Felt very tired.

The area at Ramree was 75 per cent mangrove swamp and a lot of these swamps were infested with salt and freshwater crocodiles. We all swam on the island but only where the water was clear. On the Tuesday one of the lads went down where the ships were and the water was quite muddied. It was a place I would never have swum myself. He was drowned there. The lads that were with him tried to hold him from going under but they said there was something pulling at him. An expert on the island said he'd been taken by a crocodile. He was one of our squadron, a real nice bloke, worked on a farm. You're told in training to keep your eyes open. We had a lecture about it. We weren't too far from the mangrove swamp and you could hear it at night, it comes alive then with all the creatures; there's a tremendous amount of noise. When the Army landed they drove the Japanese into the swamps and the crocodiles killed hundreds of them. They used to call the crocodiles the allies.

*Tuesday 13th Feb. 1945*
Pretty terrible today. Joe Prior drowned in sea, can't find body yet. Wrote to Olive. Gun post again.

*Wednesday 14th Feb. 1945*
Joe still missing, Went swimming in sea. On guard.

*Friday 23rd Feb. 1945*
Wrote Olive. Day off. Went to see Paddy at 22 C.Cs. He got a dose of malaria. Buried a G.I. over at cemetery. Still no mail. Night in bed thank God.

When we'd finished up at Ramree we were sent to Cox's Bazaar in India and this is where we were when we heard they'd dropped the atom bomb. They said it was a big bomb but we didn't know quite what it was.

When the war ended out there everything went mad. The authorities suddenly found they had a situation. We'd got Malaysia, Singapore, Hong Kong, Indo-China, the Dutch East Indies, all these areas that were *loaded* with Japanese prisoners. The only Japanese I ever saw were prisoners. There were two types: the coolies and the educated. The coolies did as they were told and were no trouble to us. If you did have any trouble you'd just go and tell the equivalent of a sergeant major and he'd knock the poor devil to the floor and virtually kick him to death. They were very cruel to their own troops.

My squadron, 2837 Squadron and 2739 Squadron were sent over to Sumatra. Our job was to get all the Japanese out and hold it until the Dutch arrived. The locals wanted their independence and we were warned that they'd started causing mayhem, they didn't want the Dutch back. We had strict instructions to keep out of that. We tried very hard to get the Indonesians to understand that we weren't there to stop them having their independence, that it was nothing to do with us. We were only there to do a policing job until everything settled down. It's terrible, but in the end we had more casualties in Sumatra than we did in Burma.

The POWs were mainly civilians. I saw the kids as they came out the prison camp. They were proper native, never wore shoes. We used to give them all our chocolate. They were nice, the kids were. It was surprising how well they could speak English. They used to come and sit on your bed and talk to you.

It was a very tense time in Sumatra. I actually felt fear for the first time there. Everybody was getting on edge. The biggest fear was of being attacked. We were so far away from any help, just by this little airstrip. We were in an enclosed barbed-wire area.

*Monday 24th June 1946*
No mail. Didn't write again and am feeling really

**157**

down for things are getting very dicey here now. No shooting tonight but had hardly any sleep. Lost appetite, could do with some leave badly.

*Tuesday 25th June 1946*
Mail. Olive/mum/Babs/Don. Made an effort to write and not very satisfied with it but must try and tell how things stand. Hope she understands. Shooting again tonight, God, when will we be out of here?

There were about 100 of us and a few huts. We had tents and what they called bashas made of palm leaves. Fifteen of us would sleep in one, off the floor on wooden beds. At night the locals would hang around the outside of the wire and throw things just to keep you awake, just to keep you frightened. If they had attacked us in numbers we would have been in trouble. We had a bloke who was so bad with nerves that he used to sleep with a cocked gun and loads of tin cans all round his tent so if anyone went in he swore blind he would open fire. He gradually got worse over the months. They took him down to the hospital in the end. I think quietly we all suffered from nerves.

One night about forty Indonesians attacked our camp. Six of our lads were involved, three were killed. The raid upset us all. I served with the men in my flight from the day I went in at Blackpool until the day I came out. One of them went in the same day as me. He was one of the lads who they went for that night. While they were attacking him in his bed he managed to turn the bed over, roll underneath the flaps of the tent and then ran like hell to get help. He ran the whole length of the airfield in bare feet, with just a pair of pants on. He was from Birmingham. We stayed together right through to the day he left, and I still phone him now. He's a smashing bloke.

One of the lads who died had only got three weeks until he went home. The frightening thing was it could have been me. It had been a matter of him or me going to Pedang. I went in the end because my number was much bigger than his for demob so they kept him back at the camp and sent me. If it had been the other way round it could have been me killed.

*Frank had become engaged to Olive one week before leaving for the Far East. They wrote faithfully to one another during their two-year separation.*

You'd get a postman on your squadron who would come round with your letters. We used to get them in batches. You'd go two or three weeks without anything and then you'd get a pile of them. Lovely. Beautiful. I would write longish letters, I'd got so much to say, but all I wanted to know was if she was all right and that everything was OK. Over the two-year separation, apart from when I was coming home there were just three bad weeks in Sumatra when I didn't write to Olive. The writing cemented us together. I don't know what I'd do without her.

Much as I wanted to come home and see her it didn't pay you to dwell on it. I saw blokes getting in a

**159**

terrible state because they wanted to go home to their girlfriend. I think it was very important to know they'd be there when you got back. Olive used to say why some girls went with other blokes: she said you gradually become very misty. I was one of the lucky ones. I never even worried about Olive. Most of the lads talked about missing their girls, we all missed them, but are you going to sit there every night and say, "Oh God"? I knew I was going to see her again. Unless I was unlucky.

*Olive describes Frank's homecoming to Coventry.*

It was six days before Christmas. It was bitter. They said afterwards it was the coldest night of the year. You forget what they look like and waiting for him at Coventry station that night with his dad I thought, "I won't know him, I won't recognize him." He was due in at seven o'clock. He wasn't on that train so we waited until about eleven o'clock and they said there wouldn't be another train that night. We walked to his home in Hillfields and I'll never forget it, but the bed: all they had was a real cold sheet, no blankets, and of course I hadn't got a nightie because I'd had no intention of staying so I slept in my underskirt. Anyway the next morning I had to work at the Alvis and I got up and I said to his mum, "I might as well go to work." I was in the kitchen having a wash and she shouted, "Ooh! There's a taxi." So of course in he walked. My hair wasn't combed or anything. I recognized him straightaway.

*Frank had nightmares when he first came home.*

I had a bad one when I'd been home about five weeks. My mother said to me, "You had plenty to say last night. What was the matter?" Apparently I was shouting and swearing in my sleep. She never told me what I was saying but my war was nothing compared to others.

*Olive remembers Frank's nightmares about snakes.*

He woke me up one night and he was sat up on the pillow with his legs up like this. He'd got the sheet and he just went "*woosh*"! He cleared the lot, blankets, bedclothes, everything went. He was checking for snakes. He was trying to look under the bed for them once and he fell. He hit his hand on the wardrobe and cracked his thumb in two places. The lady doctor at the hospital asked, "How did you do this?" "I fell out of bed" he said. He didn't tell her why.

*Frank has been a member of the Burma Star Association for about seventeen years.*

They're great guys. We don't care what your rank is, so long as you served in Burma. You're treated the same no matter if you were a colonel or a private. We've got some wonderful men running it. Their children are doing it now, sons and daughters. You've always got somebody there, men who've experienced it. I'm the welfare officer. If anyone's sick I'll go and visit them, see if there's anything we can do. We might send them away on holiday, get them an electric wheelchair, that sort of thing. We've got a memorial tablet in St Margaret's Church on Ball Hill. I put the names of any of our branch members who have died on to the roll of honour. I designed the board and we had it made out of Burma teak. Yesterday afternoon I was putting a name on, one of our lads had died. There's over a hundred names on there. There's only about thirty of us left now.

I go to the Memorial Park on Armistice Sunday. I stand up on the Cenotaph and say the Burma Star Prayer to the crowd. How can you feel other than a bit emotional? A lot of good men died, a lot of nice men. All I hope is that it wasn't a total waste. I look around and I say the prayer and I wonder, "What do all these people think now, all these years on?"

# For the Purposes of this Operation You Are Considered Expendable

## The Story of Ernie Sherriff

Ernie Sherriff volunteered for the RAF in 1941. After contracting German measles ("very unpatriotic") and getting as far as flying Tiger Moths in his training, Ernie served as a rear gunner and was posted to the Far East in 1943 where he flew on bombing raids against the Japanese.

The only reason I volunteered was the two blitzes on Coventry. I lost my grandad, two uncles and so forth. We were a little bit unhappy about that lot so I joined the airforce. I joined in 1941, but because I was working on aircraft they put me on deferred service. I kept writing to them and plaguing them and they fetched me in around December time when I was about eighteen.

I went to the Far East in 1943. We stopped in the Middle East, then travelled down through Aden into Bombay. There was a bit of jungle training there, live off the land type of stuff, if a monkey will eat it you can eat it, and shown how to. In Burma it was conditions you were fighting as much as the enemy. They were pretty primitive, but we were better off than a lot of the Army people.

There'd be a couple of crews, that's about fourteen men, in a basha, which was a hut made of bamboo and palms. You had a charpoy, which was a wooden bed: four posts, four runners, string, there's a base for a mattress and then the canvas piece went on top of it. It was quite comfortable, but when you got back from an operation you couldn't sleep for two or three hours anyway because you could still hear the noise of those bloody engines in your ears.

Insects were a pest. Damn nuisance, they really were. They used to give you tins of malaria cream, it was bloody useless; it was to keep mosquitoes away, but your mosquito net was as good as anything. There were plenty of spiders but you took no notice of them. You'd get these big beetles, they made an awful noise like a buzz bomb when they dived. It was such a clout if you got hit with one of those. The biggest nuisance we found were the white ants, termites. I took my greatcoat off the wall once and I left the back of it on the wall. The front fell off on the floor in my hands: they'd eaten half my coat! That's why I had to have a new logbook, my blue one got eaten. I left it on the floor when I came back from a raid and when I got up in the morning they'd got halfway through it. That's why when the Indians build, they always put a layer of dung

**164**

underneath before they lay a base because the termites won't come through it.

You'd have to check your boots for scorpions; you'd even have to check that they hadn't crawled under the aircraft. Damn nuisance. Our basha was at the end of a jungle path which led down to the aircraft. Me and this chap Reeves, who I was at school with in Coventry, we were coming down this path and he said, "I've been here for six months now, Ern, and I've never seen a snake yet."

I said, "You're walking round with your eyes shut."

"How do you mean?" he said.

"There's one right in front of you."

"I can't see it."

I picked up a pebble and threw it and a little cobra came up. I told him, "You make enough noise when you go down the path and they get out of your way. Look up there." There was another one, a green tree snake, wrapped round an overhanging branch. "I wouldn't have seen that," he said. Basically I'd been there longer than him and we were lucky because our navigator was a French Mauritian and he was used to dealing with snakes, so he used to go along and point them out to us.

Our toilet was only a bamboo screen with a bit of a hole in the ground and a board to sit on. We went out to the toilet one night and I was going along when this navigator, who always used to carry a cane with him at night, suddenly said "Stop!" A couple of steps in front there was a big three footer, a cobra. He went "tap, tap, tap, wallop" with his cane and killed it as easy as that.

Another time we came to check over the aircraft one morning and there was this little python wrapped round the undercarriage. A Ghurka comes over and out comes his cookarie knife. Off comes the snake's tail, he grabs its head, lops that off and unwraps it from the undercarriage. He cut this cookarie straight along its length and tore all the skin off. They ate that snake. I had some of it myself that night.

We flew off from a number of airfields, some from Burma and others north of Calcutta up towards the border between India and Burma. We were all over the place really. We would target bridges, railway lines, that sort of thing. If you couldn't get through there would always be a secondary target. If you couldn't get through with mines, you had to jettison them or bring them back. Our targets could be anywhere from Bangkok upwards, but the majority were in Burma. How often you'd go off on operations would depend a lot on the moon and we'd go night and day, depending on when we wanted to hit a target.

I would be straight in the back, underneath the rudder. You were too busy to think a lot of the time. You were over the sea, fairly low level; you had to keep out of enemy radar and so forth and keep your eyes open for anything else that was going on. You didn't think much about death, that was something that happened to other people. You might think about it afterwards but you don't at the time. I always had a little ivory elephant on the top buttonhole of my battledress. That was my mascot, I always had it with me and never flew without it.

If it was a very long trip we would go to an advanced airfield close to the bomb line and take off and refuel then, so that we would get the longer range once we were over enemy territory. The longest one I did was nineteen hours. We were sent off to mine the harbour just outside Penang, because there were Japanese convoys supposed to be heading that way. It was the only time we ever went through a drum head service because they didn't expect us to come back. They told us at the briefing that for the purposes of this operation we were expendable. They just say those words to you precisely: "For the purposes of this operation you are considered to be expendable." How did I feel? We had a lot of faith in our commanding officer, he really worked everything out to a T. We were overloaded, our fuel tanks were stocked up and when we got to the end of the runway he told us before we took off, "If I don't get off, none of you are to try it." About fifteen Liberators went off on that operation. We got there, dropped the mines and we all came back. We had nineteen gallons of fuel left, not enough for a full circuit, we had to come straight in but we made it.

I did lose friends. If men were known to have gone down, all the kit would be taken away while we were sleeping. That was a very disheartening time when you woke up in the morning and found the bed next door all stripped off, blankets, kit and everything all gone. You'd often find out someone was gone when they didn't check in the same time as you did. Most of you should have been back within half an hour, three quarters of an hour. You'd all gone off at the same time, hit the same targets. Unless you'd force-landed somewhere else, you'd wonder where they had got to. I knew of one crew that went down by a railway line and they were all executed. That was the Japanese for you.

I think my hardest time was when we were hit and on fire. We'd let our bombs go and took two direct hits. One engine got taken out and there was fire in the tanks. We managed to get it out but we had to force land. We were able to cross the bomb line and we went in at Cox's Bazaar. I was soaking wet from petrol where the fuel had come down the tanks. It was just luck that we survived that. I was even surprised when we went in that the aircraft didn't go up in flames. They dragged it away and it wasn't repaired so we had to wait at Cox's for a few days until they came and picked us up.

*Ernie was sent home to England at Easter in 1945.*

I was in Bombay General Hospital with dysentery and malaria. I had them both in the same hospital, it was quite common to have them both together like that. You weren't on top of the world. I didn't lose a lot of weight but I had an eighteen inch waist! I came out and they put me on a boat and sent me home. I was supposed to be going back to Tiger Force, the bomber wing that was going to be formed to raid Japan. I ended up being sent up to camp at Catterick and then on indefinite leave for a while. I wouldn't have minded going back to Burma.

The Burma Star Association is so important to me because I've got an awful lot of friends in it. We were all forgotten together over there. We had to rely on one another because you couldn't rely on anybody else. All the supplies, even a lot of the aircraft we got in the early days, were what they were getting rid of over here. When they'd worn the aircraft out, we got them. Mountbatten came over and stopped it and made sure we got the new ones. When I came back nobody wanted to know. As far as everybody was concerned the war was over, but it wasn't over. The war with Japan was still on and it carried on right until August.

I don't think people remember the war nowadays, we're still forgotten. I've got four sons and if my own children asked a question I'd answer it, but I didn't push it on them. I don't want them to be interested in war. It's a dirty business. Of course, all four went in the Navy.

There was a hell of a lot of difference between the German enemy and the Japanese. The Japanese were an enemy who wouldn't give way. Basically if you were shot down over Germany you could expect a reasonable amount of fairly decent treatment; you couldn't expect anything over there. I get on well with the Germans, I've got German friends, but I can't forgive the Japanese.

# They Looked Like Skeletons

## *The Story of Ken Alcock*

Ken Alcock served nearly seven years in the Army in postings all over Britain, Africa and the Far East, where he spent several months in the Burmese jungle mending equipment sent back down the line by infantry troops.

I was called up in 1939. The Army were totally unprepared at that point. They got all the old uniforms out and that's what they gave me: a greatcoat, tunic and riding breeches, would you believe.

At one point I was stationed in Cornwall along with a contingent of ATS. We had a tragedy happen there. There was a German plane on its way back from a raid over Bristol and he'd got a load of bombs left. He flew over our camp and dropped them, destroying about three Nissen huts and killing fourteen of our lads along with twenty of the ATS. I was on the burial party which carried these bodies in makeshift coffins to a local church. We dug the graves for them. A contingent of Cornish boys filled the gaps in our regiment then.

I'd been writing to my girlfriend, Mary, in Coventry. I'd known her since we were children. I was stationed in the Scilly Isles when the city was blitzed. The news wasn't very good and I didn't get much information; I just had to wait to hear from her. When I did she told me her aunt and uncle had been killed. They lived at 53 Mickleton Road in Earlsdon and Mary was at no. 51. I'd visited her at the house all my childhood. No. 53 had suffered a direct hit and the dividing wall between the two houses had come down. Mary's family had hidden under the stairs. They were virtually buried in there, the piano was up against the door. An air raid warden came and they got them out eventually. She told me a team from Hereford came the next day and dug her dog out from under the sewing machine table where he'd hidden. He was still alive.

*After being stationed around Britain for some time, Ken did a six-month course in Derby and joined the Royal Electrical and Mechanical Engineers.*

We were sent to Nottingham to be drafted overseas. When we got there they didn't let us out at all because when people were going on draft there was a chance they could disappear, just abscond. So they were always calling us out on parade to count us. You'd no sooner get back in than they called you out again. The officers would come round: "Get your hair cut!" I'd just had a haircut this particular day and that barber was bloody awful. Along comes the officer, "Get a haircut!"

"I've just had a haircut, sir."

"Well, get another one then. And take his name!" I had two haircuts in two days and the thing was, you had to pay sixpence for it!

They issued us with two kits: one for cold weather and one for the tropics. They didn't tell us which one we would be using. Every few hours you'd have a kit inspection and have to lay the whole lot out. It was to keep you on your toes and make sure you didn't abscond. I'd had about thirty-two injections at some point; the vaccination for smallpox made me really ill.

The day came when we had to get on these trucks. We didn't know where we were going and we ended up in Scotland where we were put on this Dutch liner. Talk about sardines. They really crowded us on. There were about five holds on this liner and the bottom ones were sleeping quarters for us men. This is where I came across class distinction and it puts you off officers for the rest of your life. There were signs, "Officers and gentlemen this way", and they had cabins. There were gates on board so you couldn't circle anywhere near their accommodation.

The conditions down below were atrocious. Hundreds and hundreds of hammocks slung on hooks, all touching each other, right at the very bottom of the ship. The kitchens for us men were down below too and the stench of the food used to come up the funnel, ooh, it made you feel so sick.

There were toilets on the deck but they weren't very nice either. I slept on there one night and I got friendly with a chap who had been in the London Philharmonic Orchestra. He always used to carry his violin everywhere with him. He used to play for us, he was very good. That night I slept on deck I was as sick as a dog. In fact we were sick nearly the whole of the first week.

We were in a convoy of about a dozen ships as we went down the Mediteranean. It was broad daylight when we were attacked by German dive bombers. We were on deck and we heard this "tat, tat, tat" and one chap on our ship was machine-gunned dead. We were lucky though, because some ships in the convoy were quite damaged and the ship next to us sank. We felt absolutely sick over that. "It could have been us," that's the thought at the front of your mind. After that happened we slept up on deck for the rest of the journey. We didn't want to be right down below at the bottom of the ship anymore.

*After a long journey Ken eventually reached Mombasa and Nairobi where he was transferred into the East African Army.*

In Nairobi I was the only man in our camp who had a pith helmet. The adjutant said to me, "Get that thing off, it should be under the bed, that hat should." They gave me a slouch hat instead. Being in the East African Army we were what they call colonial serving officers and so we had the status of officers, and if you were above the rank of sergeant you could have a batman. So I had this chap, Sylvester, a very nice bloke. He would keep my kit clean, make the bed and things like that. One day he hadn't made the bed, so I said, "Sylvester, you haven't made the bed." I saw him later with bamboos and poles and he was actually building me a bed. "I didn't mean that," I said, "I just meant you to tidy it up." He was a lovely chap.

*After leaving Africa, Ken moved into India and his final destination, Burma.*

When we got to Chittagong in India we were shocked by how terrible it was. There was sewage in the streets and it was totally disease ridden. There were rats and snakes; I'd never seen so many snakes in all my life, great big ones too. We made a camp just outside the town and everybody came down with diarrhoea and malaria and whatnot. I'd hung my coat up in our hut and when I opened it up there was a big rat hanging off the inside and it had eaten all the lapels off the coat. We were glad to get out of there.

Just after leaving Chittagong the riverbanks were infested with Japanese troops, so we had to keep a very watchful eye as we sailed along. Every now and again the boat would get stuck in a sandbank and we would all have to move across to one side and try and tilt it off. We got trucks when we reached Imphal. Mine didn't have a handbrake and we had to carry this big rock inside the back of the vehicle and put it underneath the wheels every time we stopped.

The insects in that part of the world are two or three times the size of the ones we're used to. There's a great big flying beetle which flies in a straight line. We used to play badminton with them. And ants! You've never seen

**174**

so many ants, millions and millions of them all over the place, and spiders — big ones — up the trees, on the branches, on the ground. We had to take anti-malaria medicine. You were up on a charge if you forgot it, that's how serious it was. Never mind killing mosquitoes, it nearly killed us. We went all yellow, everybody looked jaundiced, but it was a good protection.

It was so hot too. A friend of mine actually died of heat exhaustion, just dropped dead right in front of me. I'd just done two sketches of a tiger and I'd given one of them to him. He sent it off to his girlfriend, but by the time she'd have got that he'd be dead.

Five or six o'clock in the morning was the time to work, it was cool then, but after that it was too hot to do anything. If you wanted to wash your clothes, you'd get a bucket of water, give them a rub through, put them over your tent and before you'd got anything else out they were bone dry. It was that hot, the sweat just used to roll off you.

George Formby came round all the gunsights in India and he gave us a cracking show. Noel Coward — his name was mud. He just stayed in the Officers' Club in Calcutta the whole time. George Formby wouldn't stay there.

I used to write to Mary from the Far East whenever I could. You'd write on this special form which was then photographed into micro-dots. That way they could send thousands of letters back and save on bulk. When they arrived in England they were enlarged again. Mary always said my letters looked like

**175**

photographs. They were always censored, of course. I wrote one once and I put "I'm fed up with this bloody war, I'm fed up with the officers and everything." It went in the post and next thing one of the officers came up to me with my letter and said, "You can't send this!"

"It's all true," I said.

"It might be true, but you can't send it" he said. "Write another one. A nice one."

Even in peacetime no natives will live in the Kabaw Valley in Burma, it's too dangerous. We went right through the lot of it. I was with the East African Army, there were about a hundred of us men just behind the infantry troops. The infantry had watches, compasses, binoculars, and when they broke they were sent back along the line to me. I was an instrument mechanic and it was my job to mend equipment like that for the men.

We were in the jungle for about three months. When we'd got so far in there was a mix up with communications and we weren't getting any food through. The Americans contacted us and they arranged to drop supplies. They used to send Dakotas over to drop food by parachute and the American packaging was very well done. Sometimes the Japs used to get it, though.

At first we didn't think much of the enemy, but we realised very quickly that they were no pushover. There wasn't a front line as such because the Japs were all over the place. You never got a good night's sleep, you dozed off and you woke up, it was all fits and starts. We'd sleep on a ground sheet when we were on the move. We used to tie it around our legs at the bottom to stop the insects crawling up. You couldn't relax in the jungle at all, you couldn't take your clothes off, you daren't. A lot of Japanese apparently got stuck in rivers and the British Army had to treat them for leeches that had infested their skin.

There was no clean water for a long while so we had to use water from ditches and rivers to make things like tea. The water looked like tea before we even touched it. We used purification tablets, but people were ill all the time in the jungle. I had absolutely terrible diarrhoea at one point and of course you just had to go wherever you could. It was awful.

Once we set fire to two Japanese. We heard some noise in the night and we fired back into the dark. The next day we went to have a look at what had happened and there were two dead Japs in a sort of shelter. Well we didn't want to touch them because we knew they could be booby trapped. They would often get a grenade, take the pin out and put it underneath a body so that if anyone touched it they would get blown to pieces. We knew all about this business. So we set a match to the shelter and left it burning. When we got back to camp that night it must have blazed up a bit more because all the ammunition they had started exploding. It was like a fireworks display in the jungle.

We came across a little clearing once. There was a table laid out with a meal for the Japanese officers. They'd scarpered and left this table complete with all the food set out on it. It was the same thing, though: booby traps. We daren't go near it and just left the whole scene untouched.

The Japanese were shockers. I was in a place once and came across a Jap hospital. They'd killed all the patients because they didn't want them taken as prisoners of war. Oh, it was grim. We thought they were a right shower. They made life hell for the Burmese people. I've mellowed a bit in my feelings now and they never did anything to me personally, but I did see what they had done to a lot of other chaps because I had to travel on a hospital ship from Bombay at one point.

This ship was half full of our soldiers who had been badly treated by the Japanese. They were all mental cases. Suicidal. They had been treated appallingly and it really struck home when you saw them. They looked like skeletons, bones poking out. All these very disturbed men were in sort of wards on the ship and all the senior NCOs, and I was one of them, had to take it in turns walking among them reassuring them that they were safe now, that no-one was going to hurt them. Every now and then someone would report they couldn't wake a man up. Some of them died on that ship, you see. We buried four of them on the way back down the Mediterranean, their bodies went over the side into the sea. It's a bit of a bad memory.

Before they dropped the bomb we were earmarked to go to Japan; the Gurkhas trained us in unarmed combat and how to kill a man. We were taught all sorts of dirty tricks, how to fall, how to attack, if anybody pushes you how to go with it and then at the final moment give it some of that! These Ghurkas were only little chaps, but they were so strong and such lovely people. This killing business was quite deadly and I can still remember a few of the techniques even now.

You always knew, it could be any day for you, that death might not be far away, but it didn't worry you all that much. You hadn't got *time* to worry and if you did fret you'd make yourself ill. You just carried on and learnt to be optimistic by nature.

I was all over the place in the war, but Burma was the worst part for me personally. It was rotten. At that time the war in Europe had finished and we sort of had the feeling "What are we doing out here?" Everybody felt like that because they were having celebrations in London and we felt as if we'd been forgotten, that we were fighting a war on our own.

Before I got home we were at Ranchi, India, for a while. They said, "We'll give you a group number for demob: first in, first out." I was in group twenty-five and they started on group one. You had these lectures, "When you go home, the Government's got plans for you. Everyone who has been in a theatre of a war, especially round here, will get first chance of a first-class council house." When I did get home I made enquiries and they said, "You're joking. There's a mile list before you."

"They told us we were going to get preference," I said.

"No," he said, "You're at the bottom of the list." By the time I got back from the Far East the excitement had died down. People were finding out the difficulties with housing and things by then, so there was no great welcome.

I served one month off seven years and I've got medals from the different theatres of war, but the one I cherish most is the Burma Star.

# Cowboys and Indians

## The Story of Norman Smith

Norman Smith had already served two years in the Home Guard when he joined the Royal Marines aged eighteen. He was a gunner on Landing Craft Support Medium in Burma.

I'd no need to join up because I was an apprentice in a tool room, a reserved occupation, but I saw my cousin in his uniform and I thought, "Ooh, I'm joining up." They didn't want me to go at work, told me I'd no need, but the boss said, "If this lad wants to fight for his country, let him go." I'd only been in six weeks and had the bad news that my mother was poorly. I got leave to visit her but it wasn't for long, and four or five days after that I had another telegram saying she'd died. That was very upsetting for me, but life went on.

I was sent down to Devon on manoeuvres and in one incident we'd been out for about two days and one night. When we got back to camp a general came to inspect us. We had to fall in on parade and as he came to me he asked me my age.

"Eighteen, sir," I said.

"Now tell me the truth," he said, "You're not eighteen."

"I'm eighteen, sir."

He turned round and said, "Sergeant major, take this man's name and number and find out how old he is." I never heard any more about it.

We were eventually sent up to Scotland where I was based on HMS *Glenearn* and we started training for the landings in France. It was getting to the end of May and we kept getting postponed on our journey down south. Then lo and behold, on 2 June they sent us on a week's leave. Then we got a telegram: do not come back for another week. Of course, 6 June was D-Day and us lads were left where we were. When we got back to ship we were kitted out with tropical gear and the next thing we were sailing to India.

Not long after we'd arrived we had to stay at this camp. The conditions were terrible, it was like a bamboo city. You could be sitting on a latrine, they were all made of wood, and the Indians would come round and empty the pans from behind you with you sitting right there doing your business. They had a rat plague while we were there and everybody had to be inoculated. That was the worst injection I ever had, a real nasty one. Everyone had a huge scab on their arm afterwards and it left a bad scar. It knocked some of the lads right out.

To get water you had to dig holes by the river edge and make sure it was boiled before you used it. I remember going down to the river with two other lads carrying these big water containers, and we saw this huge snake by the water's edge, it was massive. One of the lads picked up a stone and threw it at the snake and it shot off. "We're not going near that water," we thought. As far as insects and snakes went, we had to carry a razor blade round with us at all times. If you were bitten you were told you had to cut the bite and suck out the poison, or get a mate to do it. If you got food from the galley these birds, kitehawks, would swoop down and steal it. We learnt our lesson very quickly with them. Shitehawks we used to call them.

My boat wasn't very big, about as long as an average living room. There were six of us on it. I was the gunner. I had a twin-point five gun, a turret one and so we could do 360 degrees. There was the coxswain, the stoker, the signaller and the gunners, and each of us was trained to do the others' jobs, in case anyone was injured. We had a mortar smoke bomb in the forward that could throw up a smoke screen in case we wanted to escape anywhere.

We used to do one silly thing on our boat. There were crocodiles in the rivers, but we would dive down into the water and see how far we could get. We'd bring up mud from the bottom. I went completely deaf doing that. I was put on a motor torpedo boat for a few weeks after that until my hearing had cleared up. Other than that I was quite lucky healthwise. One of my mates who used the same bunk as me when we were sleeping in tents was always getting malaria. He would get quite poorly with it, go all yellow.

My first encounter with the Japanese was at a small choung (that's a sort of tributary of the main river) in Burma. We had to drop these two intelligence officers off near the Japanese lines. We sailed from our base for about one and a half hours and then tied up to a tree. They jumped off and disappeared. We were just about to make a cup of char when a mortar shell dropped by the tree. One of the lads leapt off, untied us and we got going across the other side of the choung. As we were making our escape we realised the whole mouth of the choung was being covered with a line of mortar shells. We waited until the last one had dropped and then made a dash for it. We were all so young. Incidents like that, sometimes it felt like cowboys and Indians.

On another occasion there were some Japanese holding a bridge over a choung. A small motor torpedo boat was going out to meet them and they needed volunteers to join the boat: four on the port side and four on the starboard side. We sailed up the choung at two in the morning, all very excited. Halfway down all hell broke loose. The Japs had seen the boat and we were sitting ducks. The captain didn't dither about. He reversed the engines and we were back in the main river in no time, saved. You were so worked up at the time and everything was so fast. You didn't have a chance to think about your situation. We were all so eager.

A couple of weeks later it was us on the attack. We had news that the Japs were trying to escape up the Sitang river so we sailed to our positions on the mainland side and waited for them. We were told to take no prisoners at all. We were briefed very strongly that if the Japanese got near you they dropped hand grenades into the boats, and under no circumstances were we to get close to any of them.

We had a very busy night firing for quite a while. You could only see shadows, but anything that moved you shot at it. It's hard to describe it, but as daybreak came we saw the damage that we'd done. The Japs didn't look a pretty sight. They were lying here and there, some of them floating about. There had been a sampan that was full of them and most of those men were dead or injured. We tied the sampan to our boat and took them further down the mainland to the Green Howards who were involved in the attack on the land and we handed them over to them. We didn't have any contact with the Japs as we pulled them along. They were quite badly wounded, I remember one who'd had his buttocks shot right off. But as I said, we didn't get near them because of what they might do.

I was doing my washing when I heard that they'd dropped the bomb. I knew it was an atomic bomb, but we had no real idea of the seriousness of it. I thought I'd be sent straight home but, no such luck. I stayed in the Far East for another year, making landings on various islands looking for any Japanese. There were one or two and they were just handed over to the Army. They never gave us any trouble. I was guarding one and he gave me his watch. I gave that to my brother and he went and lost it! The Japanese prisoners would always be bowing to you, showing a lot of respect.

We picked up European and Eurasian prisoners of war too. We'd pick them up off the islands and drop them off in Singapore. They made our lives so pleasing because they were so glad to be going home again. Some were going back to Holland and they'd go over the moon for a bar of chocolate. I've got no grudge against the Japanese, but I can understand other people who do. I know someone who was a prisoner of war in Singapore and he was ill treated. They used to push sticks down his nails and set them on fire. I can understand people like that hating them to hell. I would have done myself, but I have no reason to personally.

When I eventually got home I was about twenty-two. They met me at the station and they had a welcome home sheet up back at the house. I wanted a new life, I wanted to forget about the war. I'd missed nearly four years. Other teenagers had had their life, I hadn't. I had to make up for it! After about a week's leave I had to get down to it. I went to my old works and everything was there ready for me. It was a little strange to start with, but then you get back into the routine.

I'm in the Burma Star and the Royal Marines Associations and when the lads get together you get that comradeship back that you used to have during the war. We're dropping off now and in about ten years it could all come to an end, but headquarters say as long as people are coming, the Associations will keep going. As far as war is concerned, they're all fighting over a bit of land and nobody wins in the end. It's pointless. It's like me fighting the man next door for his garden and I've already got one. It's just greed, greed and envy.

# PART EIGHT

# PRISONER OF WAR

# There's A Man in Here Who Comes from Coventry

## The Story of Arthur Adams

Arthur Adams was called up for Army training at the very beginning of 1942. He served in the 7th Battalion of the King's Own Scottish Borderers who were then taken into the Airborne. A lance corporal, he was in the first glider to land at Arnhem on 17 September 1944. After being wounded Arthur remained a prisoner of the Germans until the end of the war.

There were no parachutes when you flew in a glider. There was a Jeep, a trailer and six of us men. I was no. 1 in charge of the Vickers machine-gun. We all had numbers, you never used a name on the battlefield. No. 2 fed the guns off the bullet belt, no. 3 was the ammunition carrier, no. 4 the water carrier and no. 5 the Jeep driver. We left England at about ten in the morning. I can't speak for the other lads, but of course I was scared. The only thought in my mind was "What am I going to meet over there?"

We landed at half past one in the afternoon. We lost the nose wheel, the two main landing wheels and the skid. The glider's nose ploughed right down into the ground until we stopped. All the dirt was being churned up inside the glider and we were at an angle of about 25 degrees, tail up. How we weren't hurt I'll never know. There were woods either side and a great big grassy area. Our job was to secure the place for the parachutists. The first thing was to get straight under cover. We'd not been down long when someone started firing at us from the left-hand corner. Of course, we started firing back, all hell let loose. I kept thinking of my family, my parents and my wife, Phyllis.

We had to wait for the rest of our lot to get together in the woods. We had orders to move on the Monday and I was packing up the gun, but an officer came up and told me I had to stay at the landing zone to cover the lads who were parachuting in. I had to stay in those woods until the Tuesday. Late that afternoon I packed the gun up. The six of us were walking down a cart track looking for a new position to set up in again. I was in the middle with two men either side of me when I was shot. It was right in my lower left leg. I couldn't see where the bullet came out so I put it down to a dum-dum bullet, the type which explodes.

We'd been told that if we were wounded, we would just be left, as it wouldn't be possible for anyone to pick us up. So my men had to leave me and carry on — I was left behind on my own. We had also been told that it was very unlikely the Germans would take prisoners. I thought I was simply going to be shot by the SS. So I sat there, alone, firing going on around me and I waited to be shot or, possible but unlikely, to be taken prisoner.

I had bandaged my leg and given myself an injection of morphine to kill the pain when I saw four Germans in between the trees. I recognised the SS insignia on their big coat lapels and remember thinking to myself, "Arthur, that's your lot." I really did think that would be the end for me.

These four SS men came towards me and said "Kaput". I knew what that word meant: "finished". I sat there waiting for them to kill me when they walked away. I had my watch on and I timed them. Those were difficult minutes. There was firing going on all around, I didn't know what was going to happen to me. I wasn't sure if the SS were going to come back, but thirty minutes later they did and they were carrying a chair and two poles. They motioned to me to stand up and I shook my head, because I couldn't get myself up. So these SS men picked me up, put me on the chair and carried me to the main road. My mind was going haywire.

There was a Tiger tank in the road and they lifted me on to the back of the tank behind the gun turret and took me to the hospital at Arnhem. That hospital was spilling over with wounded from all sides, but they couldn't treat me there, so I was taken to another hospital in Utrecht, about 10 miles away. The SS had left me by now, of course, and these tank people were pretty rough. All along this 10-mile journey you can imagine what I was thinking: "Any time now they're going to stop and finish me off."

When we got to Utrecht they literally kicked me off the back of the tank outside the hospital gates and left me there. I couldn't walk, I couldn't get up so I waited until somebody came and picked me up, and that was the start of my prisoner of war life. I was twenty-three.

An abscess started to form on my ankle because of all the congealed blood from my bullet wound, so I was taken to the surgery in the hospital. This German surgeon told me to lie belly down on a table and then he stuck a needle which — I'm not joking — was about 12in long right down my leg into the ankle and he burst the abscess. I'd had no anaesthetic and it was absolute agony, I was really shaking. I had my arms wrapped round the table during the procedure and was holding it so tightly with the pain that I still had big marks on my arms two days later. When the doctor turned me round afterwards I looked straight into his face: "You German butcher," I said. I wasn't scared to say that to him, it just came out. He said to his orderly afterwards, "I will not see this man again." He called me a man and not a soldier because I'd called him a German butcher. Mind you, I thought afterwards: he did the job, he drained the abscess and for all I know, if he hadn't I could have lost part of my leg.

We had to take three different hospital trains to the prison camp at Munich, because the RAF kept attacking them. They didn't know the trains were full of POWs of course, there was no Red Cross on the side. They machine-gunned the engines. The first people to run were the German guards. They hared across this field away from the train and we all followed. I'd never seen so many plaster casts and crutches in my life. When you're under attack by planes you forget about your wounds, suddenly you can run! I only had one crutch and there I was running across the field with the rest of them.

I was sent to Stalag 7A near Munich. It was a five-storey building and every time the RAF came it used to sway like a pendulum. My prison was a work camp, and when I was passed fit I had to go on a working party to lay the railway lines that our RAF lads had blown up. Some mornings we would actually be out there working at the railway station when the RAF were bombing. Now that goes against the Geneva Convention but that's what happened.

We'd walk out to the station and nine times out of ten you'd get German civilians throwing buckets of water over you and shouting a bit of abuse. They were still nasty right up till the end. The guards would do nothing at all about it. We had to walk past a concentration camp too. We could see what was going on because the prisoners would cling on to the railings and you could see the state they were in, so thin and terrible looking.

There were about 150 of us British in the camp, but there were already Poles, French and different nationalities inside when we arrived. They told us the things we could do and the things we couldn't. For instance, you weren't allowed to look out the windows. You could open them but you weren't allowed to look out. A guard would follow you wherever you went: if you went to a different room, upstairs and downstairs, if you went to the toilet. The toilets weren't very clean — you can imagine 150 to 200 men, oh dear.

You could have one shower a week but you couldn't shave. I didn't shave from the day I was wounded until the day I was liberated, you couldn't because you had no gear except a piece of German soap and a towel. We must have stunk but we never noticed.

You slept on a straw mattress, had one blanket and used your clothes as a pillow. In the winter you had to sleep in your clothes to keep warm, it was that cold. Most of the guards were all right but there were one or two sadistic ones. I remember one in particular. He'd lost an eye at the Russian Front and we called him Bog Eye. If you didn't do what he said he would be quite happy to hit you with the butt of his rifle. I never got hurt myself but one of my mates didn't do what Bog Eye wanted one time and he got beaten with the rifle butt.

One day a guard came and stood in our doorway. "There's a man in here who comes from Coventry," he said in perfect English. My mate on the bunk above looked at me and I held a finger up to my lips. "I *know* there's a man in here who comes from Coventry," this guard repeated. My mate said to me, "You better say something." So I put my hand up and went to him in the doorway.

The guard said, "I'm sorry to frighten you but I used to live in Hinckley." I thought, "Is it a catch?" But no, he really had lived near Coventry for most of his life and had been repatriated when the war started. This particular guard told me that if I ever needed anything he would get it for me and he did. He used to bring me German sausage and stuff. If they'd found out he would have been shot straightaway. I used to share everything with my mate. You would get sauerkraut from Monday to Sunday and I hated it. When I got back home, it was a joke with my wife. "Would you like a nice jar of sauerkraut?" she'd ask me. "Ooh," I'd tell her, "you can stick that!"

Sometimes there were arguments among us men. I mean, we were all locked up together and you were under terrible tension. A prisoner has only got two thoughts: "Home" and "Are they going to shoot me?" You would be like that all the while. You were on a knife edge. Every prisoner there felt tense all the time. We used to sing a lot to keep our morale up, "Roll Out The Barrel" and things like that.

Whenever the Allies advanced we moved camp, but on May Day 1945 the Americans came to liberate us. Bog Eye had already scarpered by then. There were about 150 to 200 guards, but when the Americans came in, three-quarters of those Germans disappeared. I looked everywhere for the guard who had been kind to me. I wanted to be good to him now that our situations had changed, but he'd gone too.

An officer came into the barracks and asked us how we'd been treated. He said to us, "Get out there into Munich and enjoy yourselves." So we spent about a fortnight doing that. Mind you, we always went in groups, we never went alone. We'd go to the beer cellars and rifle wine and spirits, stick bottles up our jerseys and inside our jackets, go back to the billet and have a ball!

We were eventually taken to a little camp in France and there was a barber there and I shaved my beard off at last! Coming back home there was just one thing on my mind: seeing my parents, Phyllis and her parents. Everything else went by the board.

*Arthur's wife, Phyllis, remembers the man who came home.*

I had a letter which gave me the bad news about Arthur. They told me that my pension would eventually stop and to take it that they didn't know for sure where he was, that he was missing and believed killed. I was told that if I heard anything I was to let them know.

I had to wait three terrible months until I had news of Arthur. I got a letter from his padre telling me he had been taken prisoner and that he'd been wounded in the left calf. Of course I thought the worst and imagined he'd lost his leg. Whenever I went to the cinema I'd watch the newsreels and every time they showed footage of prisoners of war the men looked so thin, they were just cages with sores all over them. I was only a young girl, I thought Arthur was going through the same thing and it worried me terribly. I used to refuse to eat. If my husband wasn't eating I didn't want to either. I found it very hard, not knowing what was happening to him.

I cut a map out from the *Daily Mirror*, that showed all the prison camps in Germany, and as the allies advanced I used to mark the camps, imagining where Arthur was being moved to. When I knew he was coming home we had all these plans. We had flags hanging out the window and we were making a banner which said "Welcome Home Arthur". I had my hair in curlers ready for the big day. What did he do, he came home a day early and there I was in my curlers!

He was a different man. When he went into action he was a picture of health. He'd always been big and strong with a huge wide neck, quite dashing in his airborne gear with his helmet and revolver. When he came back he'd lost three stone. I used to cry. I wanted to feed him up. I remember crying when he wouldn't eat my rice pudding. He had a few blackouts as well. I remember him collapsing at the pictures. They said it was shell-shock or stress.

*It took Arthur a while to adjust to civilian life.*

I was released from the services when I got home. "Unfit for Army requirements," they said. For months and months when I used to go out with Phyllis I was always looking behind me. I couldn't relax at all. It took some time for me to get back to normal.

Do you know, the day after I landed in Holland the bagpiper arrived and he marched up and down playing "Blue Bonnets Over The Border". He was the man we all had to congregate round in battle and the man who got us going. It gave us courage.

Sixty-one years on if I hear the pipes playing it still fills me up and takes me back to those days. I get very emotional.

# The Worst Three Weeks of My Life

## The Story of Jack Forrest

Jack Forrest was a flight engineer in the RAF who flew on bombing missions with 619 Squadron over Germany and France. On D-Day they flew to Caen in Normandy, but in the early hours of 7 June, returning from their thirtieth mission, Jack and the crew were shot down by enemy aircraft and only two of the seven men on board survived. Jack was one of them.

*For some of his time as a prisoner of war Jack kept a wartime logbook which had been given to prisoners by the Red Cross. During a twenty-one day death march before his liberation, many things were thrown by the roadside, but Jack managed to keep hold of this diary and extracts from it are included in his story.*

The noise of a Lancaster with a full bomb load was absolutely terrifying — completely ear splitting. That was the worst bit of it. You feel as if you'll never get off the ground. If an engine cut you'd had it. I was always

**199**

with the same crew and we'd been through a lot together. My skipper was Kim Roberts, an Australian the same age as me, twenty-one. We crashed at East Kirkby once when we were flying back from a mission over Berlin. It was half past three in the morning, we were at about 130mph. I didn't know anything about it; I just felt a bang as we came in and I hit the clocks and dials and whatnot and was knocked out unconscious. I finished up a deep blue colour from my head right down to the tips of my toes. The rear gunner's gun turret was ripped right off and he was actually found up a tree very badly injured. I never saw him again.

When you went out on the bombing raids it was a case of *they bombed us, now they're getting a little bit back*. You never really thought too much about what you were doing; if you did think about it you wouldn't do it. I remember when we were bombing Berlin, it was the worst target of the lot to see: aircraft blowing up above me, below me, German fighter planes, anti-aircraft shells, lights and flashes. The whole scene was just like Dante's *Inferno*. It was terrifying.

On the operation I was on at Nuremberg, ninety-six of our aircraft were shot down. The losses in bomber command were horrific. You'd see a plane go down in the dark and think, "I wonder if I know him?" When you came back you went straight into debriefing and they'd mark off the crews as they returned. You'd soon realise who hadn't made it. You'd talk about it — poor so-and-so, wonder if he survived, if he was a POW. Nobody thought it would ever happen to them, only that it might happen to somebody else. Everybody thought like that.

We took off for our twenty-ninth mission on the morning of D-Day, returned successfully and flew back in for a night operation in the early hours of 7 June. We'd dropped our bombs over some bridges outside Caen and were on our way home when all of a sudden the wireless operator said, "I think we've got a fighter behind us." He'd picked something up on his radar screen.

The rear gunner said, "I can't see anything."

"I'm sure there's something behind us," the wireless operator said again.

Then all hell let loose. Cannon shells were hitting us, gunfire, three engines burst into flame within seconds and I heard screaming at the back of the plane. You don't have time to think, you just act automatically. The only thing in your head is "Oh my God." My skipper, Kim, shouted "Abandon aircraft!" We had our parachutes on. I bailed out along with Reg, the bomb aimer. We were the only ones who made it.

My parachute harness opened, I came down in the darkness and in a few seconds I was on the ground, we'd been flying so low you see. The Germans had flooded areas of Normandy and I landed in about 5ft of water and was soaked through. It was quiet and there seemed to be no Germans around. I started shouting "Reg! Reg!" Eventually we found each other. The first thing Reg said to me was, "God, and Vera's pregnant again."

We buried our parachutes and made our way to an orchard. We were both wet, but I was absolutely sopping, so we had to hang our clothes out on the trees and bushes to dry them and sit there in our pants; luckily the cigarettes were dry! It was light by now and we could see a house in the distance all on its own. Reg's surname was De Viell, and as his clothes were dry and mine weren't I said to him, "With your surname you must be able to speak French. Go up and see if there's anyone to help." He found a French farmer but he just wasn't interested. He kept saying "Boche! Boche!" and didn't want anything to do with us.

You always had a little sort of escape kit when you flew a mission and one of the things we had in it was a map. We decided to try and make it to Cherbourg, moving at night and laying low in daylight, and we did that for three and a half days.

We didn't have much to eat at all, it wasn't early enough in the season for apples and things. We had the odd Ovaltine tablet and water purifying tablets that we could use, and we found a few strawberries. We would hide in bushes in the day. We were doing this one afternoon and decided to creep along a bit. We saw these two Germans coming on bicycles. We stopped in the hedges and lay down flat. Lo and behold they stopped right next to us, got off their bicycles and had a fag. Then they got back on their bikes and rode on their way. If only they'd known there were two British airmen hiding on the other side of that hedge.

*Jack's diary, 1944*

We pushed on for about five hours with a rest now and again to recover our wind and trying to get a bit of strength back. I myself felt more like crawling on my hands and knees than walking. I had never gone so long before in my life without eating and I was feeling it very keenly. My stomach felt as if it didn't belong to me and I wanted to be sick although there was nothing inside me to bring up and a headache didn't help any.

On the afternoon of the 10th June we could hear German voices in the area so we decided to get mobile and try and move on. We were crossing a break in the hedgerows when all of a sudden there was a voice, "Achtung!" We put our hands up and a load of German paratroopers ran across to us. Daft as it sounds, it was like playing cowboys and Indians when you were a kid . . . We had a drink of water then had another march of about one and a half miles being guarded by a bloke on a mule armed with an automatic pistol (Schmeiser, similar to the American submachine-gun) and a soldier walking behind us with two revolvers pointing at us.

We asked for food but it never came until our guard had his evening meal or tea, which consisted of a hunk of black bread and piece of butter and some of the German coffee which is made of acorns. He gave us a piece of his bread and butter but told us if anyone saw us eating it he would be in trouble. As hungry as I was it took me about fifteen minutes to get a half slice of it down me, it was vile stuff.

These paratroopers didn't treat us too badly, they didn't knock us about or anything. They took us to a farmyard and put us in a pig sty, gave us some water, which we'd asked for. Then they marched us along this road to a château. When we went in the entrance we saw this tree with a dugout around it and in the trench sitting at a table was a German colonel. When we marched in, he said "Good evening, gentlemen. Sorry to see you in this predicament. Would you care to join me for a drink?" Those were his actual words and I've never forgotten them. He was very polite, had been educated at Cambridge and spoke perfect English. He asked us to sit down, we had a glass of wine with him and quite a chat. We said to him, "This won't last long. You'll soon be defeated." He told us, "No, we've got some secret weapons that we're going to release very soon. I'm not going to say any more." We didn't know about it then but he was talking about the flying bombs, the V1s and V2s. Then he said, "I'm sorry, but now I've got to put you in with some of your compatriots."

We were taken into the château and put with eight American prisoners from the Airborne who had been dropped at Normandy. There were five officers, all doctors, and three sergeants who were medical orderlies. This château was being used as dressing station and the American prisoners were taking care of the wounded. We slept on the floor that night and were woken up the next morning by the place being bombed by American aircraft. We weren't treated too badly there, we were allowed to help ourselves to carrots and onions from the gardens.

*Jack soon found himself having to deal with German battle casualties.*

*Jack's diary, 1944*
We had to give a helping hand with the wounded troops who were being brought in to be patched up a bit, then bundled into a truck and sent further into France to a proper hospital. There were some very sad cases of shelling coming in, blokes with legs and hands and arms missing and internal injuries. I felt very bad myself from just seeing their wounds at first, but I got hardened to it in a few days and it also gave us all the satisfaction of knowing that our soldiers were doing something at the beachhead.

We had to bury a German soldier while we were here. What a burial, he was a good big young Hun of about 22 and he got in the way of some shell splinters — he bled to death. We buried him in the local graveyard, wrapped in a bloody blanket under four feet of soil. (Incidentally, when we left Périers which had been frequently strafed and bombed by P47s, we noticed that a bomb had fallen on the graveyard near where we buried him, so all our hard work was undone and he was blown from his resting place.)

*From this first place of imprisonment Jack was moved about from place to place and camp to camp,*

**205**

*sometimes enduring the dangers of aircraft attacks when he was on the move.*

*Jack's diary, 1944*

Our march led us through the town and we had a glimpse of what the P47s had been after, it was the railway station and it was just no more: a terrible mess. We had to wind our way in and out of bomb craters here as well. While we were doing this 12 more P47s appeared and circled around us, everyone began waving handkerchiefs, bits of rag and anything handy to try and tell these pilots we were prisoners and not Germans. Two of the kites came down very low and had a look at us without firing and we felt safe, then 2 more came down straight at us and when about 200 yards away, fired their guns. Everyone at once scattered, and I fell flat on my face (my feet refusing to move). I lay there for not more than ten seconds, then I was on my feet and into some nearby thickets where I lay panting and huddled into some bushes till I thought the strafe was over. It was and everyone was cleaning up and looking [for] pals etc. I found Reg and Jack after a few minutes, they were both OK except for a few scratches. Luckily no one had been hit — only shaken up a bit. The jerries had us line up again to be counted, this took nearly an hour and at its conclusion it was found that 7 Yank officers had escaped. (Good luck to them.)

They put all airmen in solitary confinement and that happened to me for a week in Frankfurt. You're in a room 8ft by 5ft. There's a bed and that's it. You didn't get any smokes, not too much food. Then they drag you out and sit you in front of an officer. "Would you like some coffee? Would you like a cigarette?" All very polite. Then they would just ask us loads of questions. All you could say was "I'm sorry I can only tell you my rank, name and number". I think they were trying to find out about radar more than anything. They wouldn't hurt you.

By the end of July I reached Stalag Luft 7 at Bankau, close to the Polish border. The first thing I saw at the gates was a chap I'd been billeted with in England. "Jack! Jack!" he was shouting. He'd been shot down too and was the only survivor from his crew. It was a new camp and at first there was six of us crowded into this little box-like hut. There was a pump for washing in the middle of a quadrangle and at night there'd be a big line of naked men waiting for a go of the pump. We could see them building the proper camp and after a couple of months we were marched down and billeted sixteen to a room and the conditions were much better. There was a stove so you could make tea or coffee, you could have a hot shower once a week; the toilets were better too.

The majority of the guards were OK. We were counted morning, afternoon and evening. We used to get American parcels and Red Cross parcels. We were supposed to get one a week, but it didn't always happen like that. I got my wartime logbook from the Red Cross. We used to make little cupboards out of the parcel boxes. We'd put them up round the walls to keep things like soap in but the German guards would come in and knock hell out the place, pull all the boxes down with their rifle butts. I've still got a little RAF badge I made out of bits of thread and a needle and cotton from an American parcel.

We could write home once a fortnight on these little postcards they gave us but I never got a letter from home. The British had sent them back to England and the mail was waiting for me after I was liberated.

There were different societies in the camp: the Welsh Society, the Scottish Society, we even had a concert party. There was what we called "a man of confidence". He was a Canadian whose family were German and had emigrated to Canada, so he could speak good German. He would act as our go-between. There was a British Army captain who was a padre too. You could go to lessons as well. I went to French classes and a lot of men went to economics because they thought that would be the next big thing after the war.

I remember one meal we would call "whispering grass". It was all the bits of vegetables the Germans didn't want to eat, turnip tops and that sort of thing, all boiled up together. We would get one loaf to divide up among eight men, so you'd just get this little piece to last you all day.

We left Bankau on 19 January 1945 at half past four in the morning. We knew we were going to go on this march, they told us the Russians were coming. We were warned that for every man who tried to escape, they would shoot ten. We felt terrible at the thought of what was ahead of us — horrible.

*Jack's diary describes how news of the impending march effected a minor panic in camp with some men looting the food store, music room and sports supplies as POWs adapted equipment (including a football split down the middle and worn as a hat) into protection against the freezing winter weather.*

### 17 January 1945

Chaps were all over the place with cricket bats, footballs, accordions and other musical instruments. We are in a bit of a mess trying to pack our kit and I find I have to discard a lot of the stuff I have accumulated since I came here. We must carry only what we have to besides our blankets.

Our division leader has come round and told us that Peschel the German security officer has stated that he will do his best to find us barns to sleep in at night and that if one man ecapes five others will be shot.

Everywhere was snowbound with temperatures down to −13 degrees — freezing. We'd packed up what we could for the march — a blanket, clothes. I didn't have many more clothes to take with me than what I've got on talking to you now. I'd made myself a sort of bonnet out of bits of RAF clothing and I'd got a bit of lambswool on my ears. It was better than nothing but it didn't do a great job. After about 2 miles everyone had dumped a load of stuff, books and things they couldn't carry. Whoever came behind us must have thought it was Christmas.

We had to walk and walk with hardly any food, some days we didn't get anything at all. The Germans didn't have that much themselves. We had snow if we were thirsty. We slept in barns, wherever we could. There were 1,500 of us: British, Canadians, Australians, New Zealanders. It was my lowest point in the war. I had frostbite on my hands, my feet and my eyes. We were in such a state — frozen, hungry, exhausted. We were told that if we stopped and sat down, we would feel all warm and that was a sign you were dying. We just kept going. I thought about my family all the time.

Once or twice when the weather was really bad and we were absolutely shattered the Germans fired their guns off to make us get up and march again. You didn't want a bullet in you so you went. At one point they came across a horse and cart and they did put some of the weakest men on that. What happened to them I don't know. We all helped each other, you leant on each other's shoulders, held each other up. The camaraderie was great.

*Always nagging at the men's minds were the questions of where they were marching to and how long the journey would last. Jack's diary gives a terrible sense of the everyday struggle which the men endured and in particular the bitter cold which they suffered without respite.*

210

*21 January 1945*

The march this night was a nightmare and the most terrible cold I ever experienced. Boots were frozen like clogs, many chaps were collapsing and frostbite had taken its toll on them before the wagon at the rear could pick them up. Eyes would not keep open and I was walking in a daze. Jack, Jim, Reg and myself took turns with helping a Canadian along for 11kms. He had just had enough and could hardly stand.

*28 January 1945*

Weather conditions at practically blizzard stage. At midnight it was impossible because of snow drifts and we were in single file for long periods. Coldest yet, snow on eyebrows freezing and covering eyes making it extremely difficult to see. With no gloves, hands just hopeless. German road transport at a standstill. Passed dead girl in snowdrift.

For part of the journey they put us on these cattle trucks, fifty-eight men to a truck. It was so crowded you couldn't lie down, you just squatted with your knees clenched up. There was straw on the floor and a steel drum to use as a toilet. That was full in no time. You can imagine the smell. They wouldn't let us out at all, we were locked in day and night. We travelled for three days like that. We didn't get much to eat: a slice of bread. At the end we all had dysentery. I'd lost 3½ stone in twenty-one days. We were all the same, we were all in that condition.

Throughout that time we kept our spirits up. There was still a lot of laughter. You know what young people are like. We had no energy for singing, but you could be next door to death and there would always be somebody to make a joke. Mind you, they were the worst three weeks of my life. We ended up at Luckenwalde, Stalag 3A, 25 miles south of Berlin.

## 8 February 1945

The first thing was to get us deloused. When we eventually took our clothes off and had a look at ourselves it shook us rigid. I had lost what little flesh I'd had before we started off and was now a shrunken skeleton of my former self. My legs and arms were like matchsticks and my face very hollow and bearded.

They gave us all an injection for typhus and treated my frostbite. The guards were all old blokes, the majority of them were all right. They were sick and tired of it by then, really fed up with the war. There were 500 of us to a block. The concrete floor was covered in straw, there was one sink about 6ft by 2ft, a couple of cold water taps. That was for all 500 men. We weren't the only ones of course: there would be another 500 and another 500, and some of them were even worse off than us. The Americans that arrived were only under canvas.

For the toilet you sat on a long pole back to back with another man. If you fell off that pole you'd had it. Don't forget, we all had dysentery. You got used to the terrible smell eventually. I can remember crawling on my hands and knees through the straw of our block and just feeling the stuff drain out of me. You couldn't do anything about it; you had no toilet paper, nothing. It was ghastly. You were past caring, though. Every man was the same. Can you imagine the stench? We all had lice too in the camps; you couldn't wash your clothes and they used to live in them. We used to wake up in the mornings and have a competition to see who could kill the most lice.

There were times as a prisoner of war when I knew real hunger. I've seen blokes fighting over half a loaf of bread. All we ever talked about was food. What we missed, what we'd like to eat. It's hard for you to understand if you've never really felt that kind of hunger.

*Jack's diary, 1945*
We talk of nothing else but food all day long. I am writing this in appreciation of mother's cooking when I was home. This life, combined with the hard time we have gone through since the middle of January, has really brought it home to me that there is nothing in this whole bloody world like home and my own mother's cooking. I think back and nearly weep when I realise how true her words have come since war forced me from home. Such things as "one day you will wish you had eaten that" or "one day you will need that instead of wasting it". I have learnt now the hard way and it has been and is still pretty tough.

Yes mum I have felt very sorry for myself when I've thought of the food you have cooked and which I turned my nose up and refused. I can't put this into words because it's an inner feeling that can't be explained. I hope my list of meals on the previous pages can be used by you on my return. I have one great wish to see our family sit around the table at home happily eating one of the meals in this book cooked by you mum.

We knew the Russians were coming, there'd been a lot of gunfire and the Germans sort of disappeared. In the morning of 22 April huge Russian tanks bashed down our barbed wire. We were chuffed, we cheered. But we didn't know what the Russians were like then.

*21 April 1945*
After a night of rumours things have started to happen in this camp. The sound of gunfire is very close and many Germans have pulled out of here. At noon the camp was taken over by POWs although the huns are still around outside. There has been a small tank action in Luckenwalde and Russians are in the vicinity. It is strange to see four jerries taken prisoner in the camp by our boys and marched to the bunker. We go to bed expecting to be relieved by morning. At 6am Sunday, there is a shout of "They're here!"

German prisoners came in droves from other places and they looked like nothing on earth. I used to feel really sorry for them. The Russians were rough on any Germans that were there. They would just shoot them out of hand if they felt like it. I saw a Russian woman shoot a German at our camp. You just sort of thought, "God, I hope that's not going to happen to me."

Our camp was 60 miles inside the Russian sector and in a way it was like becoming their prisoners. They wanted us to get rifles and follow them into Berlin. Nobody went. I didn't want to go, I'd seen enough of the war.

*Jack's diary, 1945*

After a week under Russian supervision everyone was down in the dumps again. The food was no better and we had to stop in the camp, to venture outside the wire was virtual suicide as they shot at anyone wearing a blue uniform. My own clothes were blue and very nearly the same colour as the Luftwaffe. I stayed inside.

We'd been with the Russians nearly a fortnight when we heard that some American wagons were coming through. Some of us decided to make a run for it and try and get on these lorries. Reg was married with children and most of the lads with families didn't want to take any risks and chose to stay with the Russians. I went for it when we saw the wagons coming. The Russians fired at us but we got on the lorries. I was scared, I wondered if I was going to get out alive. The men who stayed behind did make it in the end and got home a few weeks after us.

When we got to the River Elbe the Russians were there, but we could see the American flag on the other side. Everybody was shouting and waving. This Jeep came whizzing across, they had a barney with the Russians and we crossed over. It was great. The Americans are so generous. I can remember my first cooked meal: potatoes and cabbage and a 7 1b tin of chicken between us.

I always wondered about the rest of my crew on that Lancaster. There were only four graves in France and I thought a lot about my skipper Kim and what had happened to his body. In the 1980s I got a phone call from Reg. "They've found Cinders," he said. That was our Lancaster's name, "Cinders Of The Clouds". It turned out parts of our plane had been ploughed up in a field. They found the plane's number on the side, LL783, and the name "Cinders". A French farmer told what he had seen in the sky that night. My skipper, Kim, was just incinerated really.

I went over to Normandy in 1996 and we had a memorial made to Kim at last and a special ceremony for him. Not many people have got their name on a gravestone, but mine's on that one: Survivors/ Survivants: J. F. J Forrest and/et W. H. De Viell. I remember holding a piece of chain in my hand from our Lancaster. It still said Coventry Chains on it. The plane had been built in Coventry, you see. I've still got parts of the plane in my garage at home.

We'd never had a picture of us taken together, the whole crew. We were going to get it done, but then we went on that mission and it was too late. I see other people with photos of their crew and I always regret I haven't got one, I've only got pictures of me on my own. When I think back on the war the time I think about the most is always being shot down. Why am I still alive? Why did the others die? I think about Kim every day of the week, whenever I wake up. Sometimes I can get quite depressed about it. Why did they die and not me? I'll always remember Kim. You never forget.

# PART NINE

# THOSE WHO DIDN'T COME BACK

# There's Someone Missing Here

## The Story of Frederick Carless

Many people never returned to Coventry after the war and lie buried far from their homes and families. The following story, told through letters and family accounts, is included to represent those who fell.

While I was researching this book I discovered an article in an old wartime Coventry Evening Telegraph about a Dutch girl whose father had found the body of a British soldier floating in the river near his home in Holland. The daughter buried the dead man in her garden and cared for his grave. She wrote to his family in England to let them know she was looking after his resting place and perhaps that might give them some small comfort. Every day men from the soldier's regiment came and placed fresh flowers on his grave, and before they moved on they made a new cross for their dead comrade. This soldier was Frederick Carless from Coventry.

His story touched me. I managed to find the dead soldier's brother, Benjamin, who told me the *story of the young man killed in Holland all those years ago.*

Fred was my big brother. I'm eighty-two now and if he were alive he'd be eighty-four. As it is, we lost him when he was just twenty-eight. He was a hairdresser before he was called up. My father wanted us both to learn a trade: he wanted me to be a butcher, which I was for five years, and Fred went into the hairdressing. He was very outgoing, loved fishing. He'd only been married a couple of years to Phyllis and she was pregnant when he went missing. Of course he never got to know she had a little boy.

He was in Holland when it happened, serving with the 4th Battalion of the Northamptonshire Regiment. He was a good swimmer and they needed some men to swim across the River Maas. The Germans machine-gunned the water and Fred was one of those who didn't make it back. That was 1 March 1945. We didn't get told he was missing until a little while after that. My mum was in the kitchen when they came to the door to tell her he was reported missing. She was so upset, she never got over the shock. To be quite truthful, from that day on she never had very good health. She was only in her sixties when she died.

While he was still classed as missing my mum asked my girlfriend, Evelyn, to visit a Gypsy Rose Lee with her opposite Coventry Council House. It was all barren round there from where it had been bombed. The war had finished by then but my mum wouldn't give up hope that he would come home. The fortune teller told her he wasn't dead, only missing. Evelyn can still remember that.

My father wouldn't accept he was dead either until it was confirmed, and when that confirmation came it was a terrible blow, a terrible blow. They always remembered Fred but they didn't speak about him a great deal. I think it hurt too much. When his baby, Michael, was born, Phyllis would come over with him quite often and they'd all go out for a walk.

*The following letter from his commanding officer was sent to Fred's wife, Phyllis, in March 1945:*

My dear Mrs Carless,

It is with regret that I start this letter tendering my sympathy with you. Your husband was in my Platoon from the time I found this battalion over twelve months ago and during that time I found him a remarkably pleasant chap who was very popular with the other members of the platoon. At Christmas he organised a platoon party which involved considerable work and self sacrifice on his part, all of which he undertook with untiring energy and good humour.

One night last week it was ordered to send a patrol across a river which secrecy forbids me naming but which has been mentioned in news bulletins for weeks. Your husband was detailed to go but enemy were located immediately opposite and the patrol was cancelled. Volunteers were asked for to try and cross two nights later at a different place and your husband volunteered.

The second in Command of B. Coy, Lt Bell was in charge and with him were your husband, myself and eleven others. We embarked and crossed successfully but the hun held his fire until we started disembarking. We then opened fire with a machine-gun at a range of about fifty yards. We had one or two casualties from bullets but your husband was unhurt but at that stage I lost luck with him. I myself stayed on the enemy bank for about half an hour then swam back, the current was very strong and the river is about 50 yards wide, only four managed to swim back. Your husband, Lt Bell and the others are missing. It is thought that they attempted to swim back, but burdened as they were with clothes, boots etc, the current proved too much for them.

Again offering my sympathy and assuring you that in due course we will avenge our comrade's loss.

I remain,
Yours sincerely,
Arthur G. Smith.

*Attached to the end of this letter was another note, written five days later:*

I was not allowed to send this letter directly to you and since writing it two postal orders have been

received addressed to your husband which I
enclose. I can now state that the River previously
mentioned was the River Maas and the place of
crossing was between the village of LOTTUM and
ACREN in Holland.

Fred had his last leave in the February before he
was killed. I remember him saying, "Now, you kids
don't get married before I come home, will you?" We
got married in 1946 and I did miss him. I thought
to myself on my wedding day, "There's someone
missing here." They looked after Fred very well in
Holland, especially the young girl; she took such
good care of him. My father really appreciated that.
He and Phyllis both kept in touch with her and
every now and then we'd get a letter from Holland.
On Remembrance Day I always think, "By Jove, I
wonder what Fred would have been doing now if
he'd lived? I wonder if he'd have reached eighty-four
and still be with me?"

After VE Day, teams of Allied Armies' Graves
Registration Command searched Holland for the
bodies of soldiers buried on farms, in woods, in
gardens. They reburied the dead in graves according
to nationalities and, under the guidance of the
Netherlands War Graves Committee, Dutch civilians
adopted many of the graves and tended them. Of
course the Dutch girl, Toos Kuypers, continued to
care for Frederick Carless's grave as she had done
from the beginning.

*Extract taken from a letter sent to Fred's parents by Miss Kuypers:*

I can tell you Mrs and Mr (Carless) that the English Grave Committee have brought a new Soldiers' Cross and she told me that in the Spring all the English soldiers [will be] carried to one great cemetery and she thinks that Mr Fr. Carless go to Vinlo in the village round Arcen.

Fred was not forgotten by the men in his regiment either. The following letter was written to Phyllis Carless in 1946 by a Coventry soldier who had crossed the river with him that night in March. It seems to sum up, simply, the sense of loss and the strong feeling of remembrance that all the veterans carry round with them today.

Dear Mrs Carless,

Maybe you don't remember my name but I met you at Coventry station. I was a great friend of Fred's and I went up with him. I've been waiting to write this letter to you for a long while now but I just didn't know how to start and what to say until I saw The Daily Telegraph on Saturday. So I hope you'll forgive me.

I served with Fred in the Northamptonshire since January 1940. I was attached to the same patrol across the Maas. I also had the privilege of attending his resting place. Please believe me when

I say that it has been really well looked after. Please accept my deepest sympathy. I shall always cherish the memory and friendship of Fred.

Yours very sincerely,

F. Sturman.

# PART TEN

# THE VETERANS IN 2005

## Albert Dunn

Albert was a postman for twelve years and went on to work for Coventry City Engineers. Although his father wouldn't let him join the Navy, you'd never guess it as Albert looks more like a sailor than any veteran I've met and, like Reg Walker, has an entire room devoted to the Navy. When I spoke to Albert it was easy to see the memories of the nineteen-year-old boy at Dunkirk are still close to the surface. He is President of the Dunkirk Veterans' Association which used to have a membership of 300. "There's only four of us left now," he told me.

## Dennis Wood

Dennis went back to his old job as a gardener after the war and went on to work at Coventry's GEC for thirty-five years. I used to see Dennis a lot round Earlsdon driving his disabled scooter up and down the high street. He would always raise a hand to wave. Sadly, Dennis died before the completion of this book and before I had the chance to collect any photographs of him. His knee troubled him right up to the end of his life.

## Gordon Batt

Gordon became manager of the Daimler Company's Newcastle and Edinburgh depots after the war. He went on to fill the role of General Service Manager for Standard Triumph in Coventry, eventually retiring from British Leyland. Gordon was one of the most enthusiastic storytellers to whom I spoke. As I sat listening to him, bird after bird would land on his balcony. Gordon may not have flown any more but he still liked to be reminded of his RAF days. I'll never forget trying on his RAF jacket, wearing his hat and looking through his logbook for the Battle of Britain. Gordon was always extremely helpful and encouraging about my book and would often write me letters including little snippets of local history for me to read. He wrote his own book detailing his war years and I would highly recommend it for anyone interested in war memoirs.[1] Sadly Gordon died in February 2004. Wherever you are now, Sgt Pilot Batt, I finished the book.

## Reg Farmer

Reg was a keen artist who painted all his life. He used to be Chairman and President of Coventry Art Guild. Talking with him at his home, his pride in his Battle of Britain memorabilia and respect for the pilots who flew was obvious. When I called on him to collect

---

[1] *Sgt. Pilot 741474 R.A.F.V.R. A Flying Memoir*, available from the Battle of Britain Historical Society, PO Box 174, Tunbridge Wells, TN4 9FA.

photographs of him during the war I found his house in darkness, and was told by a neighbour that, sadly, Reg had passed away.

## Alan Hartley

Alan worked at Whitman's in Coventry as a machine-tool engineer before going into insurance. When he's not playing golf, he is a very busy man who can organise anything. He is the founder member of the Down Ampney Association and is currently campaigning for a war memorial at Arnhem dedicated to the memory of the RAF aircrew who gave their lives on those dangerous resupply missions. Alan also single-handedly arranged for the surviving air ambulance nurses who had brought injured men back to Down Ampney to attend a garden party at Buckingham Palace in recognition of their service. He has a great sense of humour and, never short of an interesting story, he was a delight to talk to and I'm sure he used to sell a lot of insurance! He played his last game of football at sixty-two and his final cricket match at seventy-five.

## Bob Barley

Bob became a graphic artist after the war. Following time as a signwriter he went into exhibitions work and eventually retired from AEC Exhibitions. He has always lived in Coventry and was married to Enid for fifty-three years. On my visits to Bob I have always been struck by his gentle and modest nature. He is a talented artist; the walls of his home are decorated with his paintings of old buildings, country scenes and, of course, aircraft. Bob is a member of the Air Gunners Association in Coventry.

### Les Lengden

Les went back to work on aircraft at Baginton after the war, owned his own hardware shop in Coundon and eventually retired from Massey Ferguson where he was engineers' storekeeper. Together with his wife, Jean, he spent fourteen years in Canada but missed home and came back to Coventry eight years ago. Les has got one of the biggest smiles I've seen, and whenever I visit him and Jean I'm always sure of a lot of laughter.

### Reg Walker

You can always spot Reg's home because quite often there is a huge England flag flying from a pole outside the front bedroom window. Reg went into painting and decorating after the war, but it was obvious whenever I visited him that his real love is the Navy. There is a whole room devoted to it, complete with ship's wheel, flags, two of his old sailors' collars and a marvellous model of his motor launch which he designed and built himself. "I made the canvas bits from my sailor's hat, something I've always regretted!" He's been married to Dorothy for fifty-three years.

### Grace Golland

For many years after the war Grace worked in Timothy White's chemist in Coventry's city centre. She met her husband Albert when she was freezing in Belgium all those years ago. They were married for twenty-nine years and had two daughters. Grace was very suspicious of me when I first called her. Like Ken Alcock she couldn't believe why on earth anyone would be interested in hearing her story. A very modest, straight-talking woman who didn't like any fuss, she always quietly encouraged me in my work with the book. Sadly, Grace died in 2002. Her daughter Linda has her mother's medal now. It's no longer hidden away in a drawer but is displayed proudly for everyone to see.

### Irene Edgar

Irene Edgar has always taught dance: Latin, ballroom, line dancing and now sequence dancing and the odd barn dance. Her oldest student is eighty-six. "I have to learn forty-six new dances a year to keep up with the teaching. It certainly keeps my mind exercised!" Irene has a wardrobe full of glamorous dresses, loves taking cruises and is a wonderful storyteller. She is devoted to her son, Jan.

### Pauline Leslie

Pauline had two children and was married to her Scottish husband, Sandy, for forty-two years before his death on Christmas Eve in 1989. She visits Aberdeen every year with her son and daughter to visit Sandy's grave. Pauline lives alone in Coventry, a gentle, dignified lady.

## John Barker-Davies

Apart from the war years, Captain John Barker-Davies has been a solicitor all his working life. After being blown up by the mine in France his hearing was never as good as pre-Normandy days, and he was disappointed when he had to give up court appearances. Every now and then I see John in Earlsdon, always impeccably dressed, with a neat white moustache. "Hello, my dear!" he says. I often wonder if the people he passes realise that he has led marines in battle against the SS.

## Jack Hawkes

When I was a little girl I used to buy my penny sweets from Mr Hawkes's corner shop at the end of my road in Earlsdon. I always knew he had a bit of a limp, but I didn't know it was because he'd been hit by a mortar bomb. After the war Jack studied at the Institute of Certificated Grocers and became a member of the Grocers' Institute. In his neat white coat he ran the family shop he was born above until his retirement. Jack has lived in Earlsdon, Coventry, all his life with his wife, Marjorie. He has one daughter and twin seven-year-old granddaughters who take over his stairlift whenever they come to stay. Jack is an eloquent storyteller and at eighty-seven still looks the same to me as he did thirty years ago.

## Arthur Mills

Like Jack Hawkes, Arthur Mills was a familiar face to me all my childhood. With his wife, Betty, Arthur owned Mills's paper shop in Earlsdon for thirty years. Whenever I visited Arthur to research his story he always made me laugh with his sense of humour. He did manage to get back to Normandy with his sons in 2001. Arthur died in November the following year and his funeral was a crowded affair. He is greatly missed in Earlsdon.

## Harold Hancox

Harold Hancox spent his working life in Coventry's car industry where he was employed by Rootes and Chrysler as an analyst. He met his wife Maureen when he was fifteen and was married to her for forty-seven years until her death in 1992. "You never quite get used to living alone," he told me, "and I still miss her." He has ten great grandchildren, including a set of triplets. Like many of the veterans' homes, Harold's house is dotted with memorabilia and photographs from his time in the war, and yes, Harold is the "Hank" who saved Les Ryder's life in the sand dunes at Alamein.

## Les Ryder

Les worked as an engineer all his life. After retiring from Jaguar cars he ran his own workshop, specialising in cylinder heads, for nearly thirty years. He had many friends in the motorbike community, and if anyone needed their bike to go faster Les was the man for the job. Up until recently he worked one day a month at the Yeomanry Museum in Warwick. Les passed away in the spring of 2005. He and Harold Hancox remained good friends for the whole of his life.

## Alan Roberts

While I was researching this book I always referred to Alan as my Sean Connery veteran because he is just as handsome and charismatic as the James Bond actor. After the war Alan spent a good deal of his life working in universities in South East Asia, where he became Dean of Engineering and Architecture. Eventually he returned to Coventry where he still lives with his beautiful Chinese wife. Now in his eighties he tells me he has his abseiling equipment ready in case there's ever a fire in his high-rise building. I have fond memories of Alan holding me in a death lock in my living room as he demonstrated killing techniques one day.

## Frank Rushton

Frank Rushton was senior lecturer in interior decorating at Birmingham College of Art and the Brooklyn Technical College for twenty-six years. After all his letter writing during the war, Frank and Olive are still married fifty-eight years on. Full of life and very friendly, Frank is welfare officer of Coventry's Burma Star Association and is the man you'll see standing at the Cenotaph in the city's War Memorial Park every Remembrance Day, reciting the Burma Star Prayer.

## Ernie Sherriff

Ernie worked as a fighting vehicle fitter at the Alvis in Coventry for thirty-one years. The Kohima Epitaph hangs on his living room wall along with paintings of the plane he flew in. He has lived in Radford, Coventry, for fifty-four years with his wife, Rita. Ernie was one of the founder members of the city's Burma Star Association and has been its chairman for many years.

## Ken Alcock

Ken was manager at Underwood Typewriting School in Coventry. He could never quite believe I was interested in listening to his story. "No-one's really been interested before." He's a very friendly man and I remember him suddenly appearing from a room in his house and plonking his slouch hat, which he'd worn in India and Burma, on my head. Ken and his wife Mary had known each other since they were children and he still misses her terribly since her death in 2003. These days he lives in Nottinghamshire near his daughter.

## Norman Smith

Norman worked for Bretts Stamping Company in Hillfields, Coventry, until he was sixty-two. He is in his eighties now but there is something youthful about Norman — you can still see the boy who went to Burma in his face. He is president of Coventry's Burma Star Association and has been married to Freda for thirty-six years.

## Arthur Adams

After the war Arthur worked for Jaguar at Browns Lane and Radford as a power press setter. Wherever you look in Arthur's home you see Arnhem memorabilia. Pictures of Second World War gliders hang on the walls, poppies collected over many Remembrance Days stick out from picture frames and a large painting of the hospital at Arnhem, the one which had no room for Arthur, hangs in the hallway. "It's my shrine," he told me. "My Arnhem." Arthur still lives in Coventry with his wife Phyllis whom he met when he was fifteen years old. "Even when I got back from the war and caught her with her curlers in, she was still my princess, my dear, and she is to this day."

## Jack Forrest

Jack is a joiner by trade. He was employed by Jaguar for twenty years, but the best times of his working life were the seven years when he taught woodwork to young people in Coventry. His house is full of the most beautiful furniture all made by him. It was a special moment for me sitting in his living room being served chocolate biscuits by his lovely wife Glenis and holding parts of the Lancaster bomber he was shot down in nearly sixty-one years ago. Jack is an extremely generous, friendly man who doesn't look his eighty-two years at all — you can still see traces of that thick hair which was so visible in the German photograph of him taken in the POW camp.